Fly Fishing for the Compleat Idiot

A No-Nonsense Guide to Fly Casting

Michael Rutter

Illustrated by
Greg Siple & Ed Jenne

Mountain Press Publishing Company
Missoula, Montana
1995

Library of Congress Cataloging-In-Publication Data

Rutter, Michael, 1953–
    Fly fishing for the compleat idiot : a no-nonsense guide to fly casting / Michael Rutter ;
illustrated by Greg Siple & Ed Jenne.
        p.   cm.
    Includes index.
    ISBN 0-87842-313-3 (paper)
    1. Fly fishing. 2. Fly casting. I. Title.
SH456.R868 1995
799.1'2—dc20   95-6709
                                                                                         CIP

Mountain Press Publishing Company
P. O. Box 2399 · Missoula, MT 59806
406-728-1900 · 800-234-5308

To my compleat wife, Shari, the bride of my youth and best friend.

To my compleat parents, Jo and Paul, who bought me my first rod thirty-five years ago, who shared their love of wild places, fishing, and literature.

To my compleat friend, Gary, my oldest and best fishing partner.

Contents

Few things are as satisfying as catching a nice trout on a fly.
Fly fishing is the ultimate way to have fun.

Introduction

Fly Fishing for the Compleat Idiot provides painless instruction because fly casting should, at all times, be fun. If it's fun, you'll learn more rapidly. This is an enjoyable, relaxing sport, not a college course in Intermediate French or advanced calculus. True, there's a lot to learn, but becoming a good fly caster shouldn't give you a headache. Few things are difficult if they're logically explained and broken down into understandable steps.

If you're like me, you've looked at enough dull textbooks and obtuse how-to manuals to last several lifetimes. This book will explain what you need to know in easy-to-understand steps. You will progress painlessly from one level of fly fishing to another with a smile on your face. The concepts you'll need to master fly casting will be presented in a logical manner, proceeding from the general to the specific.

You'll learn how to cast and how to catch fish. You'll learn about flies and how to read water. You'll learn about bass and trout fishing. You'll also learn about casting for salmon and steelhead. You'll learn about fly line, how to select a fly rod, and what sort of equipment

you'll need. You'll learn how to be successful with a fly rod in almost any situation.

I'll assume that you're intelligent but uninformed on this subject. I want you to love fly fishing. I also want you to enjoy this book and the education we fondly call "learning how to catch fish with flies." What's in it for me? If you like it, you'll feel good about buying other books I've written.

I must confess that I'm a little irreverent about the educational process. Too many fly fishing folks take themselves and this beloved sport too seriously. They make it a lot harder than it really is. I've always felt that a few harmless fishing tales mingled with a few anecdotes go a long way toward explaining facts and techniques. In my experience, a chemistry teacher with a smile on her face and a good repertoire of jokes gets her subject across more effectively than one who looks like a Puritan preacher, keeps a stiff upper lip, and threatens you with flunking. Perhaps I use this example because I had to repeat Chemistry 105 several times.

Fly casting seems difficult, but don't be fooled. It's a myth that enables established

1

casters to feel like snobs. Basic fly fishing isn't as hard as some people want you to believe it is. Nearly anyone can learn—even a wet-behind-the-ears kid. In fact, the best fishing summer of my life came when I was 13. I "borrowed" my dad's rarely used bamboo rod and his cheap automatic reel. I also drafted all the flies that dear old Dad owned, swiping the plastic case that held his generic flies. I've since discovered that I didn't pull a fast one on my old man. He knew all along, but good dads are that way. In 1967, a lot of kids were taking off for the Golden Gate to follow the Grateful Dead and join the hip generation. I guess he was glad I got bit by the fishing bug instead. I fished all summer, from the Rogue Valley in southern Oregon to Star Valley in western Wyoming. I caught hundreds of fish in rivers, streams, and ponds. It took me almost all summer to lose my dad's flies. (New ones magically appeared in August, thanks to dear old Dad.) I made tippet (the line you tie your fly to) with odd pieces of monofilament. I must have slapped the water like a beaver tail. I was surely a sight. Completely untaught, I knew no buzz words, yet I caught more fish than a boy has a right to catch. My method was simple. I tied on the first fly I thought looked pretty and cast. Sometimes I caught fish. Other times, I didn't catch fish. It was hit and miss, but it was fun.

After a wonderful 13th summer, I spent the next 15 years reading fly fishing material and feeling like a complete idiot. I had no background in the vocabulary, so I got bogged down with all those stupid terms. I had no foundation. I only knew I liked to catch fish with a funny, long rod and funny, thick-green line. It was sort of mystical. I tied on a fly and hoped. I knew I needed to know why I was doing what I was doing, but I wasn't sure where to start. I started to feel like I had no right to catch fish, because my form was so bad. It began to shake my confidence. But I finally quit blaming myself. I was catching some fish, so I was obviously doing something right. I knew the problem wasn't my poor reading ability, since I was working on a graduate degree in literature. I knew there was more. I wanted to learn, but I barely got past the maze of meaningless buzz words and the snobby, pretentious writing style. I wanted to get into the fly casting conversation, but I wasn't sure which questions to ask.

Too often, a fly fishing book is like a freshman biology text—a book supposedly written for beginning biology students. Yet a Ph.D. writes it and another Ph.D. evaluates it for use in his or her class. Readability and the logical flow of complicated ideas never seem to enter into the picture, because the instructor has long forgotten what it's like to be an uninterested freshman whose only interest in biology involves the back seat of a Chevy. A massive dose of unfamiliar language doesn't bother the instructor, because it all seems so obvious, even clear. He's forgotten that at one time he had to learn from the ground up, too. He says he wants his students to learn, yet he expects them to pick up biology from a text that's way beyond their level. It's no wonder so many of us bombed freshman biology (and chemistry). It's no wonder that most of us are baffled by fly fishing materials written by experts.

While fly fishing might seem complicated, it's really quite simple. You're trying to invite a fish to feed on your offering. You're trying to get it to eat artificial food. The important thing to remember is that the food must look good. If a fish is content but dinner looks absolutely perfect, you might tempt him to take a look. If all is right with your presentation, he might take a halfhearted bite. If the fish is in an aggressive mood, hungry, or mad, it won't make a lot of difference *what* your dinner selection looks like. SLAM! You've hooked him.

It's a good thing fish are sometimes feeling aggressive, hungry, or mad. It means that even if you slap the water, aren't careful with your shadow, wade too close, fish at the wrong time of the day, present the correct fly poorly, present the wrong fly correctly, or tie on the wrong size fly, you can still catch fish. You'll catch enough to keep you going until you learn

You can fly fish almost any time. This high mountain snowstorm caught me by surprise.

to eliminate many beginning mistakes. As you improve, you'll no longer be catching just aggressive, hungry, or mad trout, but content and selective trout—fish you've really fooled. And you'll be doing it consistently, because your presentation of the artificial dinner will be okay, then good, pretty good, damn good, sort of perfect, almost perfect, then perfect.

Some people think fly fishing is difficult because if you really push the sport, there are few limits. Fly casting is an infinite series of plateaus. There is always another technique to work on, or one more strategy to perfect. But the bottom line (another pun) is this: after a few minutes of practice and with a simple understanding of the basic principles that govern the whole affair, you can catch fish. Even an awkward cast can result in fishing action. At 13, I made a lot of mistakes, but I still brought fish home.

When I teach someone the finer points of fly casting, from one idiot to another, I spend half an hour in my front yard. We go over a basic cast, a couple of strategies, a knot or two. Then we're off to the Provo River. Chances are very good that the new fly caster will be into a trout, or at least a strike, within 20 minutes.

While basic fly casting isn't difficult, it *is* the most complicated way to fish. It's not like going to K-Mart, buying a closed-faced $12 reel, slapping on a worm, and heading off to catch the pale-silver planters at the slime-filled local reservoir. There is more to serious fishing than just getting fish. You've got to do it with some semblance of grace, observing a few rules. If *fish* were our only objective, a quarter stick of dynamite and a match would be enough.

Maybe some would say I've become a fly casting snob, but I won't ever forget how lost I once felt. Nor will I forget that you might be starting at the beginning. You are my readers. You've paid your hard-earned cash for a book I've written. You want to learn, but you need a place to start. I intend to give you that place. I want to see everyone fly fishing. There's room for anyone who wants to join the fly casting ranks. You come, too!

Welcome to the world of fly fishing—a world of exciting adventure. As we say in my part of the Rockies, "Tight lines!"

ONE

Talking Like a Fly Caster

A Handle on the Basics

AYBE IT'S UNORTHODOX TO BEGIN A FLY FISHING BOOK BY DISCUSSING TERMINOLOGY AND A LITTLE OF MY CASTING THEORY, but I think it's the best place to start. It clears up a lot of muddy water and gives you a good foundation. It's easier to learn how to learn if you understand what people in the know are talking about.

In Chapter Four, you'll get action. I'll ask you to take your rod out to the yard (or to the nearest irrigation ditch, park, or stream) and have at it. *Fly Fishing for the Compleat Idiot* is written so that you can jump around without getting lost, since the chapters are topic-oriented.

If you can wait, leave the fly rod in the corner for the time being. Let's get you thinking and talking like a fly caster. You're going to have to endure this stuff sometime, and now is as good a time as any. It'll give you the background so that the pieces will fit together quickly.

I know you're eager to feel that rod in your hand—to make a few false casts in the front yard so your neighbors know that you are a person of consummate taste. You're anxious to feel the cool stream rushing about your waders as you drift a perfectly timed dry fly in the current above a likely pool. You want to hook a four-pound brown

and feel the rod tip dance as you pump the fish out of the strong current. You're eager to hear the reel whine as you gently palm it when the big brown takes another run under the willows.

I admit that a hands-on approach to fly fishing is best. (Even though I can't be there personally to direct your cast.)

Reading about a fly fishing adventure is second best. (Look for articles in issues of popular fishing magazines.)

Reading about how to fish is third best. (Check out the rest of this book.)

A discussion of fly casting vocabulary (in other words, this chapter) is . . . well . . . fourth best at best. I admit that this chapter is a little removed from what fly casters love to do, but trust me—it'll help.

Even as I write, my words haunt me. They are virtually exact restatements of my infamous fifth-grade teacher's famous lecture on academia. She always crowed to my class, "Of course it doesn't make sense *now*, you little beasts, but all the pieces will fit together when you're in college . . . if you ever get there, Mr. Rutter." She glared at me for emphasis. "And you *won't* if you don't memorize your lessons!"

I imagine she'd be surprised to see my office at the university.

How I hated her class. How I hated her. She always ignored the fun stuff. All she'd do was drill spelling rules, grammar rules, vocabulary rules, punctuation rules, pounding them into our impressionable young minds. She'd never say why we needed to know such nonsense. I knew 32 rules for proper comma usage, but somehow I failed to see how they applied to composition. The more frogs and snakes she found in her desk, the more tacks that materialized on her antique oak swivel chair, the more words or rules we got to memorize.

But her class was not a total loss. The majestic Rogue River ran past Patrick Elementary School. I was fortunate because I sat by a window. As she wrote meaningless words and proper usages of this and that on the board, I watched the magical salmon and steelhead fishermen work the pools of turbulent, deep green water with their ten-foot fly rods. I dreamed of being a fly caster. More than anything else, I wanted to cast flies and catch salmon. I wished I was anywhere but in her classroom.

"A certain amount of vocabulary is necessary in learning," she'd say in her frosty autumn voice after I uttered another heartfelt complaint. "You have to know the terminology to know where to start."

As painful as it might be now to admit, the same thing holds true for the fine art of fly casting. My purpose is not to cram a billion things down your throat, but to teach you enough so you can effectively enter into any fly fishing conversation. There will be no quiz. Browse through this chapter and the rest of the book. Become acquainted on a pleasant level. Think of this as an easy "Hell Week" prior to the official football season.

Fly fishing is filled with buzz words. (The pun is intended.) You can hardly even buy basic fly fishing tackle without wading (another pun) through fly casting terms. Knowing the language gives you a certain amount of power. Salespeople won't be sharpening their pencils as you walk into the tackle shop, because you'll be able to converse intelligently. They won't be able to talk you into what you don't need. You'll be in control. Buzz words are the key. Not only will they help you buy the right equipment, but they are a step toward understanding casting technique.

The Caster's Vocabulary

Each person has to decide how far he or she wants to go up the Great Fly Fishing Chain-of-Being, but it begins with a basic fly fishing vocabulary. These terms are the tools that help you enter into the conversation. Let's look at some of the terms that have plagued aspiring fly casters since the days of yore. These include specialized terms like wet flies, dry flies, wet lines, dry lines, attractors, film, sinking tip, backing, tapered leader, and others. With an initial understanding of the common "buzz words" thrown around so carelessly in the fly fishing world, you'll be halfway there. Fly fishing is a sport based on motor skills, but it's also a sport of vocabulary. As is the case with any new discipline, half the battle is won when you understand the language. Most of the confusion has to do with semantics, not technique.

The Fly. The fly itself is the fish's dinner, or what you *hope* will be the fish's dinner. The word can be confusing. A fishing fly can be something other than a fly or an insect. It can be a frog, a fish, a mouse, or nothing real at all. Feathers, fur, yarn, and other materials are tied to a hook so they will look like something a fish would eat. Flies might be tied to look like various forms of terrestrial or aquatic insects.

Terrestrials are land-going bugs that somehow fall or get blown into the water. They include grasshoppers, mosquitoes, ants, and other accidental swimmers.

Aquatics are water-going bugs that live part or all of their lives in the drink. The larval and pupal stages of a caddis fly or stone fly nymph are classical examples.

Flies can also imitate *crustaceans*, aquatic creatures with shells. These include scuds, shrimp, crayfish, and cress bugs. Or a fly can mimic a leech, a snake, a frog, or a mouse.

Exact Patterns are flies that are tied to match or duplicate an exact hatch of insects in terms of color, size, and shape. When trout are content, it often takes an exact pattern to produce a strike. For example, a Gray Wulff is an excellent imitation of a mayfly.

Attractor patterns are generic flies. They have the general size and shape of an insect, but they are not tied to look like anything specific. A Coachman pattern is an excellent example. It can be fished wet or dry, and it doesn't resemble any specific insect.

Flies are fished one of two ways—wet or dry. Occasionally, a fly, like the Coachman, will work both wet and dry.

Dry flies are fished on the *film*, or the top layer of water, which is sometimes referred to as the surface. Dry flies get wet, of course, but they're designed to float. Dry flies often mimic terrestrials, but they might instead imitate a newly hatched aquatic waiting for its wings to dry. A dry fly will have a *hackle*, a cock feather tied near the eye of the hook, to help it float. A rub-on substance called *floatant* is also used to help the dry fly stay afloat.

The dry fly.

Wet flies are fished under the surface. These flies might imitate drowned terrestrials or aquatic insects (nymphs). Wet flies can also mimic small fish, leeches, or other fish delicacies. A wet fly is designed to sink. When it's imitating a live creature, the wet fly is tied with soft material so it will look alive underwater. A streamer is an example of a wet fly.

The wet fly.

Whether fishing with wet or dry, you want to present your fly perfectly, so that it looks real in the water. That's called *presentation*.

The Same Old Lines. When you fish, you use a *line*. It's a simple matter if you're fishing with a spinning rod, because you use the same line for everything. When you fly cast, you deal with a number of different lines. The weight of the line casts the fly.

A *fly line* is more than just a line. If it floats, it's called a *dry line.* If it sinks, it's called a *wet line.* If just the front of the line sinks, it's called a *sinking tip.* And sinking lines aren't all equal—some lines sink faster or slower than others. It all depends on what you need. If you catch a big fish and it yanks off enough line, you get into your *backing*—the line behind your regular line. As if that's not enough, lines come in different sizes: a #4 line is smaller than a #8 line. Weight is determined by how much the first thirty-foot section of the fly line weighs.

On to the fly line, you tie a *tapered leader.* This is a clear, monofilament line that tapers along its length. The thicker (heavier) end attaches to the fly line. The thinner (lighter) end attaches to the fly. The taper of the line helps roll the fly over during the cast. The *tippet* is the thinnest part of the leader.

What do you suppose a *strike indicator* is? It's not something you use when you bowl.

It's a sticky Band-Aid-like bobber that attaches to your leader. It bobs when a fish takes your fly. What is a *strike* or a *strike zone*? It's not part of a thermonuclear war. A strike is when the fish hits your fly—although a hit isn't literally a hit. It's actually a mouth gulp. The strike zone is that elusive area you want your fly to float across, so the fish will see it and strike. *Tight lines?* Well, loose lips sink ships and loose lines lose fish. If you don't have a tight line, you won't be able to set the hook.

What about *drift?* Drift is when your fly floats naturally, the way you want it to float, without *drag* over the strike zone. If your fly *drags*, it's being pulled by the line. Drag is usually a drag because it spoils the perfect float you're trying to create.

Some other terms you'll hear if you hang around fly shops are *lunker, bucket mouth,* and *bonefish*. A lunker is any big fish, one you'd sell your soul for. A bucket mouth is a large mouth bass. And a bonefish is a fighting fish that fly casters dream of, a bony fish that swims the waters of the Bahamas and off the coast of Florida.

Now you have a basic understanding of fly fishing lingo. You can begin to talk like a fly caster, and you're ready to wade into the history and traditions of the sport.

TWO

The Casting Tradition
A Brief Look at Our Sport

THE HISTORY OF FISHING AND THE HISTORY OF FISHING LITERATURE is as old and as rich as the history of humans. Fish have been deified, worshipped, and wondered about. So has the act of procuring fish. The history of fly fishing and the history of fishing itself are inseparably intertwined.

As you'd expect, early-day anglers fished out of necessity. They most likely employed nets, spears, baskets, or anything that would work. The method didn't have to be pretty; it only had to work. The various spawns, when fish were most vulnerable, were likely times of great celebration. So was late summer when low water made fish easier to capture. Put simply, fish equaled food, and food equaled life.

One day someone discovered that the act of procuring fish became more than just gathering food—it became sport. The act of fishing itself was at least as fun as the act of eating.

Fishing and Literature

We know from early records that the Chinese were fishing in a most enlightened manner around 900 to 1000 B.C. In fact, they were ahead of their time. Ancient records tell of early Chinese anglers using long sticks of "thorn" for rods, silk for line, and bent iron, sharpened to a point, for hooks. On the hook, they placed bits of grain or insects for bait.

We also know from a book called the *Tchouang-Tseu*, recorded about the same time, that Chinese craftsman split and glued bamboo strips together to use as fishing rods—the early forerunner of the split bamboo rod. These not-so-primeval rods were strong and constructed primarily for carrying water pails. It's not hard to imagine, however, one occasionally being wielded as a trusty fishing pole when the handy thorn branch broke under the strain of a big carp.

Homer, the blind Greek poet, mentions fishing with a rod, line, and hook. Consider some of my favorite passages from his great epic poems: "As a great fisher on the land lets down with a long rod his baits" (*Odyssey XII*). Or "When a man on a rock drags with a line and a bronze hook the sea" (*Iliad XVI*). It makes me want to reread the classics from a different point of view. I can't help wondering if an angling man or woman ran out of grasshoppers or worms and tied a handy gull feather or some yarn from a fraying toga on the hook, thus creating the first fly. Just because it was never recorded doesn't mean it didn't happen.

Plato and Aristotle, among other Greeks, got in on the act with a number of digressions on angling and the merits of fishing. Fishing was very important to the Greeks. Fish and the act of fishing is replete in Greek history and literature. The Macedonians, second cousins to the Greeks, and famous for the conqueror Alexander, are usually credited for first documenting flies and fly fishing. And the Romans assimilated this fishing tradition into their own culture. The Romans knew a good thing—gods, literature, geometry, architecture, and fly casting.

But Rome didn't have the market covered on the fishing action. Egypt had some high-level angling going on. Early impressions on the tombs of the pharaohs and other Nile nobility show people fishing with what look like hooks—perhaps even flies. Certainly fishing wasn't new to Cleopatra. In Plutarch's *Life of Marcus Antonius,* we learn that Marcus didn't like to be outfished—especially by his lady love. The two ill-fated lovers were fishing on the Nile one afternoon, and Marcus wasn't catching much. Even worse, he wasn't impressing his Egyptian paramour with his superior Roman angling skills. In desperation, he bribed one of his slaves to brave the crocodile-infested water and attach a big fish to his hook. Cleo was impressed, until the macho Marcus overdid it. He bribed his slave with more loot to hook large fish several more times.

The trick became obvious, and Cleo became miffed that a certain expatriated Roman was so worried about his fish tally. The next day they went fishing again, and Cleo wanted to get even. This time she had her slave put a nice fish on her hook, and to make matters even more exciting, she had her slave hook some "salted fish" on the Roman's hook. She wanted to teach him a lesson. And she did. Plutarch says he took the lesson well since Cleopatra had more to offer. From then on, he paid more attention to the woman for whom he betrayed Rome.

After Rome fell, people certainly continued to fish, but few wrote about it. *The Book of St. Albans,* published in 1496, was the first major work on fishing since the Gauls invaded the empire. It made quite a splash. The wonderful book was written by a woman named Dame Juliana (a female writer was nearly unheard of in that day). Besides being an accomplished angler, she was a dedicated Benedictine nun, a prioress. Her words are delightful reading and still poignant today. At the end of her angling primer, she observes:

> "You must not use the artful sport [angling] for covetousness . . . but mainly for your enjoyment and to procure the health of your body and, more especially, of your soul. . . . You must not be too greedy in catching your said game, as in taking too much at one time, a thing which can easily happen. . . . [You] could easily be the occasion of destroying your own sport and other men's also."

Perhaps the most famous writer on the subject was the gentle Sir Izaak Walton. His

work, *The Compleat Angler*, is the most famous book about angling ever penned. Brother Walton, as my friends refer to him, wrote a number of tracts, pamphlets, books, and biographies. He made his living as a tailor, but he also had a talent for writing and catching fish. The Renaissance poet and preacher John Donne was one of his favorite subjects of study. His other love was fishing and writing about it.

In between doing business and dodging Cromwell's do-gooder protectorate, Izaak did a lot of fishing. His masterpiece *The Compleat Angler* was published in 1653 by Walton's friend, Richard Marriot. *The*

Compleat Angler sold aggressively in London and throughout Europe. Izaak expanded his narrative and updated it for a 1655 printing. That edition sold out, and expanded editions followed in 1661, 1668, and in 1676. It's required reading for anyone interested in fishing. There were fishing books before, and there have been fishing books since; however, none has captured the fishing mystique like Mr. Walton's seminal piece.

Through Piscator, his main character, Walton presented an ideal angling world. Life was simple. Everything ran smoothly, and big fish were nearly always hooked. It was the bible of angling, and still is. Besides passing on fishing lore and tips, Izaak made bold comments about men, women, fashion, and politics. He bravely proposed that fish were naturally more beautiful than women. The black spots on salmon, he suggested, give them an added beauty not given to "any woman by [her] artificial paint or patch in which [she] takes so much pride."

A Look at Rods

By the mid-1600s, fly fishing and the art of dressing a fly were beginning to evolve. Rods were still long, cumbersome affairs. Many were an unwieldy 18 to 20 feet long. By the early 1700s, some of the better rods had bamboo tips, but none had any finesse.

In Pennsylvania around 1850, a clever man spent a lot of time casting to wily trout in the limestone-spring creeks that flowed through his local hills. After a while, though, he got tired of fishing with a "small tree," otherwise known

as his fishing rod. He wanted something delicate and light to hold. Bamboo seemed well suited to the sport, but it was still heavy. He decided to split the cane vertically, hollow out the center, then fuse it back together again (a process similar to what the Chinese had done 3,000 years earlier). This process lightened the rod, considerably reduced its diameter, and gave his rod action.

The man didn't know it yet, but he had just taken the first steps toward inventing the first modern fly rod. Next, he refined the process. He split a bamboo into four vertical pieces. After he sawed the cane into strips, beveled it, and roughly fit the pieces together, he steamed each of the four strips straight. Then, he sanded the strips and crafted them until they fit together. He glued the cane and cut it into two or three sections. The ends were fused with metal caps called ferrules.

This new style of rod caught on quickly because it was light and wispy. No more fishing with a small tree.

A few years later another angler improved on the concept. He split bamboo into six vertical pieces, giving the rod more strength and a better feel. A good cane rod was varnished several times, topped off with a handle of cork, placed in a case, and sold. The craft became more and more refined. Rod makers found that the cane grown in Asia—specifically in Southeast Asia—was best because it was strong and had a high resin content. For almost a hundred years, bamboo rods reigned supreme.

After World War II, the folks with the best bamboo were politically incorrect. We had a first-rate Cold War going on, and British and American rod makers weren't allowed to speak with, play with, or trade bamboo with a communist—even if they did have the best cane. I suppose you could say we saw red. About the same time, the "miracle" fiberglass and plastics were becoming commonplace and started to fill the gap.

Fiberglass was strong and workable. It was also relatively cheap. Fiberglass rod tips didn't break like bamboo tips so often did. Except for the very wealthy, most casters switched to glass. Some glass rods, though, were better than others. The attention the manufacturer paid to the hollow center of the tube and the thickness of the walls was critical.

After glass came graphite, which was the best of both worlds. It was lighter and had more feel than either fiberglass or bamboo, and it was stronger. Bamboo is still used, but only in expensive custom rods. It has a feel of its own and a certain amount of nostalgic charm, but it's inferior to even middle-of-the-road graphite. Today, nearly all quality rods are made of graphite.

A Look at Lines

Over the centuries, a number of materials have been used as fishing lines. Anglers tried twisted pieces of fiber, sinew, silk, or cotton. The most common line in the Renaissance was made from a horse's tail. In Izaak Walton's day, it was the line of choice (although there weren't many choices). More than a hundred years later, a practical person realized that silk had a higher purpose than smoking jackets (some-

thing the Chinese had known for 3,000 years). Silk lines became popular with the more affluent casters. Later, silk and horsehair blends and cotton lines hit the scene. Woven silk lines became standard after trade channels with the Orient were opened up, and the product became less expensive. Silk isn't a bad casting line—certainly a lot better than horse hair—and it remained the line of choice halfway into the twentieth century.

Silk floats when it's dry, but after it gets soaked, it sinks. Apocryphal casting tradition has it that the greased silk line (the addition of grease allowing it to float) was an American tradition. According to folklore, a hungry caster was eating a greasy leg of lamb. The caster in question accidentally got grease all over the end of his new, very expensive silk line. But something interesting happened: his line floated nicely on the surface of the water, and he was able to fish a dry fly quite a while before his line got soggy.

If the legend is correct, the first floating line was invented thanks to an American. The slob forgot about his leg of lamb and caught tons of fish that were feeding on the surface. Half an hour later the grease wore off. The hatch was over, the angler's line and fly sunk down, and he caught tons of fish that were feeding below the surface.

Later on, different oils and greases were used to keep the line floating. Casters could now fish on the surface or under the surface as they chose.

The disadvantage of silk was that you had to dry it out when you got home or it would rot. In the early days, silk was very expensive, and it wasn't that easy to import a new line from the Far East, so anglers took good care of their gear. Another problem was mice. After you rubbed rancid grease on a line, the rodents thought it was fair game to nibble on the silk.

Today we make sinking and floating lines with plastic. To make them float, manufacturers inject tiny air bubbles into the plastic, making the line buoyant. To make the line sink to various depths, the manufacturers incorpo-rate fewer air bubbles in the plastic. You no longer need to eat greasy food to get your line to float. And, as far as I know, mice rarely eat plastic fly line.

Technology has brought fly fishing to a science. It's easier now to be a skilled angler than ever before—and, in some ways, less expensive. The important part, though, is that you are now part of the fly casting tradition. It's time for you to make your mark on the sport.

A nice brown trout caught on light tippet.

THREE

Fly Fishing Gear
Getting Set Up

ANY FLY CASTERS HAVE A DIFFICULT TIME. GET-
TING STARTED because they purchase the
wrong equipment. I won't let you fall into this trap.

All fly fishing is gear-related, so let's go over
the gear you'll need. A cheap setup may seem
like the place to start, but it will be a liability
before long. Conversely, you don't have to look
like you've just stepped out of an L.L. Bean
catalog either. Somewhere in between is an
outfit just right for you.

It's not impossible to figure out where to
start—just a little confusing. Clerks in general

sporting goods stores can't be relied upon
unless you happen to find one who seriously
fly fishes. Many know just a *little* more than
you do or, worse, they are mandated to push a
certain product line. Some know at least a few
buzz words, and all know how to casually direct you to the most expensive products (especially if they're on commission).

The other side of the retail option is the
specialty fly tackle store. Prices will be higher,
but the clerks have their fly casting ducks in a
row. They will expect you to share their pas-

*Fly fishing is a gear-related sport.
Before you walk into a store, have a
good idea of what you're looking for
and how much you can spend.*

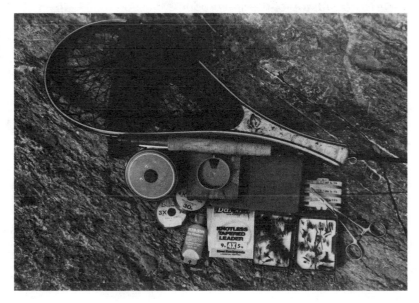

sion for fly casting. They'll be disappointed if you're not willing to mortgage your house and your firstborn to get completely set up *right now*. Such shops don't sell much middle-of-the-road equipment.

As a new caster coming into this wonderful sport, you'll have to spend a few bucks. If money comes as hard for you as it does for me, I want you to spend it carefully and get good, lasting value. Sometimes you can get off cheaply, but other times it's worth spending a little more to get something that will work and be satisfying. That's why I'm here to help you. I'm going to give you a crash course on the fly casting gear you'll need to get started.

Think of it as a modest investment—modest, that is, compared to a tropical vacation or a car. But don't kid yourself. Fly fishing isn't cheap. It's not like casting Powerbait with a $15 rod and reel combo. There are specialized tools you can't do without. Some gear you'll need now, other things can wait until later. You don't have to go with top-of-the-line products, but you do have to go with good equipment. If you can't afford what you need, it might be better to wait. In fly casting, cheap gear is only a waste of money and a source of frustration.

At the very least, you'll need a rod, a reel, a fly line, leader, and flies. Depending on where you fish and how cold the water is, you might need waders, a vest, fly boxes, and polarized glasses. Float tubes, canoes, a fancy vest, wader bags, and upgrading can come later.

What sort of fishing do you want to do? Before you look at lines, weights, reels, and rods, consider the types of fish you're after and the fishing situations you'll be involved in. How often are you going to fish? What seasons will you fish? What types of water? All this has a direct bearing on what you'll purchase.

Are you going to fish for salmon? If you are, you'll need a heavy rod. Will you fish for trout in small mountain streams? Then a light rod will do. Are you an all-around caster? If so, you'll need a "general" rod. Is the water you'll fish icy? If so, you may want waders. At the very least, before you march into a store, you'll want to have a clear idea about what sort of fishing you expect to do.

The Least You Should Know About Fly Rods

Money can't buy you love, but it can purchase a damn-fine fly rod—a rod that you'll pass down to your children. Take as much care selecting a rod as you would when you're choosing a lifelong mate. *Your selection of a fly rod is one of the most critical decisions you'll make.*

The first question is what do you want to spend? How much *can* you spend? Balance what you can afford to spend against how much you want to enjoy fly casting. Remember, you'll spend more time tenderly holding your rod in a day or a weekend than you'll spend holding the hand of your significant other in years, if not decades.

Go window-shopping. Drop into a sporting goods store or a fly shop, and pick up a rod. How does it feel? Do you like the handle? Do

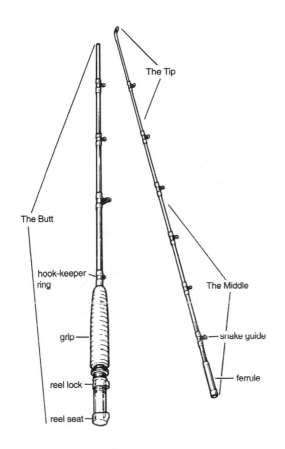

The Tip

The Butt

hook-keeper
ring

grip

The Middle

snake guide

reel lock

ferrule

reel seat

The basic fly rod.

you like how the reel is seated? Buying a rod is a marriage of sorts. If thoughtfully approached, it can last a lifetime.

Size and Weight. Fly rods vary in length, but each rod is designed for specific line weights. The rod and the line must be balanced.

Look on the shaft, just above the grip. It will say *Weight: 5, 6, 7, or 8*; or *6-7* or *7-8*. This means you should use a #5, #6, #7, or #8 weight line respectively; or you can choose between a #6 or a #7, or a #7 or a #8 weight line.

For the average person, an 8' 6" or 9' rod is the best choice for most situations. For large waters, long casting, and big fish, you might

want to go longer. For small streams, you might want to go shorter. For short men, women, and young anglers, an 8' or 8' 6" rod might be the best choice.

Unless you plan to specialize, you'll probably want to start with a #5, #6, or #7 weight line and rod. If you're going to fish small waters with good-sized but not really large fish, a #5 or #6 rod will do nicely. If you get into big fish or if you have to contend with wind, you might look at a #6 or #7 weight. Unless I'm after salmon, steelhead, or large bass, I use a #5 or #6 as my all-purpose line and a 9' rod.

The Action. Have you ever see anyone hold up a rod and shake it? It's as common in a fishing store as kicking tires at a car dealership. For many, it's a conditioned response. Why? Shaking a rod allows you to check for softness, flex, and firmness. When you're in a store or a shop, look at several rods that are designed for the same weight, ignoring the price tag for now. Make a comparison.

Softness. Put the rod together if it isn't already assembled. Give it a few modified Zorro swipes. The key word is *crisp*. Does it feel crisp, or does it keep wiggling like a thin piece of willow or lath? If it whips back and forth, if it feels loose and sloppy, you won't be happy with it for five minutes—no matter what kind of deal you cut. A rod that's too soft isn't worth a damn. During a few Zorro snaps, how does it feel?

Flex. Now check the flex. Rods have different flexes for different purposes. For your first rod, you'll probably want one that offers what's

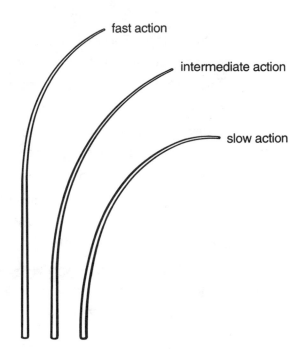

fast action

intermediate action

slow action

The action of a fly rod.

Fast action:
Most of the bend is in the upper part of the rod (the first quarter section). Many anglers prefer this rod because it casts powerfully with tight loops. This is also the rod for long casts and weighted lines. A fast action rod is unforgiving—you'll break the tippet if you set the hook too hard.

Intermediate action:
The upper half of the rod bends. This is a compromise rod.

Slow action:
This rod bends from the butt section. An effective rod for wet flies. It throws a wide loop, and the flexibility is good for fine tippets. You can feel this rod load.

called *quick action*. With a quick action rod, most of the bend or flex is focused nearer the top (or tip) of the rod, not near the bottom (the butt). A less-expensive rod generally flexes all over the place, especially toward the butt.

If you're going to fish weighted flies, a stiff rod allows you to lift the fly out of the water and keep it above your head more easily. This means you're less likely to get a nymph earring or a streamer nosepiece, or decorate your shirt or hat with your favorite leech.

Firmness. Some people refer to rod firmness as "stiffness." Rods designed for light line weights are less firm than heavy-lined rods. This is why you compare one #5 weight-line rod with another—not with a #8 weight-line rod.

Move the rod from side to side in 12- to 14-inch strokes. Start easy, then accelerate with directness. How does this one feel compared to other rods?

Now move the rod up and down. Again, start easy and accelerate. How does it feel? If the rod keeps moving and doesn't dampen quickly after you stop, you don't want it. Generally, the more you pay for a rod, the quicker it will dampen.

Don't buy a rod your first time out. Visit a few stores and go back later. After a little practice, you will notice differences. Until you can pick up on these differences, don't think about pulling out your wallet. Will the shop let you cast? Does a friend have a similar rod you could borrow for a front-lawn practice session? Be sure the rod is what you need before you buy.

What's It Made Of? *Bamboo* rods cause some casters to well up with tears and go all slobbery. From the early part of the nineteenth century until the second World War, most fly rods were made of bamboo. The best came from (and still do) a special cane called

Arundenaria anabilis, grown near the Gulf of Tonkin off Southeast Asia (the northern part of Vietnam and China).

It takes two to six weeks to make a decent cane rod. The finest bamboo is chosen and split into six pieces then formed into a blank. In the old days when labor was cheap, rods were available at every price. Nowadays, a good cane rod usually starts just under a $1,000. The rods are labor intensive, and most are "custom" affairs.

Bamboo has a distinctive feel when you cast. The cast is solid, and something whispers tradition. Many anglers feel that these rods don't perform as well as modern rods. I agree, but I love them anyway. Bamboo rods require a lot of care. If you scratch the finish or hook the shaft during a cast, you need to fix the goof right away. Bamboo has a delicate tip, so you must take special care when you're fishing with heavy flies or landing big fish. The biggest drawback is this: a fast caster has to slow down his cast and use wider loops to preserve the rod tip, which may break with speed.

However, there's no denying the traditional charm of a bamboo rod. I used a cheaper version until I was in my twenties. It was lying around the house, and I "borrowed" it because my dad didn't want me to touch his new Fenwick. This bamboo rod hangs in a place of honor on my wall. I don't enjoy casting it much, but I immensely enjoy looking at it.

For many years following World War II, *fiberglass* was the wonder material virtually all rods were made from. Glass rods were tough and lasting. In their day, they were considered

fair casters. My father's Fenwick was made of fiberglass. When he purchased it, he paid top dollar, for it was then state-of-the-art. He was very proud of that rod. Whenever he was on a house call and I could steal it out of his hunting/fishing closet, I thought I was fishing on top of the world. The rod is now almost 30 years old. It has caught a zillion fish, but it hardly looks used. It hangs on my wall, too.

The first fiberglass rods had metal ferrules, like the traditional cane rods. Ferrules were the best way to connect sections of a rod, but they created dull (dead) spots that were annoying when casting. Also, if the rod was going to break, it would likely happen where the metal met the glass. Later, a wise caster at Fenwick decided it might be a good idea to jam the end of the smaller section of the rod into the hollow tip of the next larger piece, eliminating the ferrules entirely. This improvement killed the dull spot, making the rod stronger and more pleasant to fish with.

Nowadays, though, fiberglass is used only in less expensive rods. By modern standards, glass seems clunky, heavy, and soft. The new buzz word in materials is graphite.

Graphite is made from carbon filament, and it has been used in rods since about 1975. There have been several generations of graphite rods, each getting better and better. Graphite fibers have a lot of vigor for their weight, and they're very elastic. When bent, they return quickly to their original form. Because they're so light, the diameter of a rod may not be much larger than a pencil. A graphite rod also offers great casting speed, so you can realize more distance. However, there are a few drawbacks. The biggest problem is that graphite rods are fragile.

Boron was a big draw a few years ago. Rods made from boron were lighter and more elastic than first-generation graphite. However, they were very expensive, and they were said to be dangerous because they supposedly drew lightning like a lightning rod. You don't see much boron these days. Graphite soon surpassed it.

I favor graphite. So will you. Graphite rods are a quantum leap over glass or bamboo. The rods are light and they wear well, but most importantly they have *feel*. A good graphite rod comes alive in your hand; it's part of you. As you may have guessed, not all graphite rods are equal. Select the best you can afford. When you factor in the number of hours you'll spend fishing and how long a good rod lasts, the better rod is worth the extra money.

Two-Piece and Four-Piece. I'm often asked, "Should I get a two-piece rod or a four-piece rod?"

Maybe this is a comment on my clumsiness: I've broken only one rod while catching a fish, but I *have* broken a lot of rods. The major rod killers have been the wicked tailgates of my truck or Bronco. Once, I cast poorly and smacked a tree. *Splat.* Another time, I sat on my friend Gary's rod while eating lunch. *Crack.* I've even driven over a rod. *Split.*

Those long, four- or five-foot sections of rod are busts waiting to happen. Since I've switched to travel rods with shorter sections, I've broken far fewer rods and ruined far fewer trips.

In the past, serious fly casters almost always chose two-piece rods because they offered greater sensitivity. But things have changed. A fisherman *might* lose a little sensitivity with a four-piece rod, but probably not. New-generation graphite is so good you won't be able to tell the difference, even if you get a middle-of-the-road rod. I lean toward four-piece rods because they perform, and because they're more packable (on a plane, on a horse, or in a backpack), and because I'm less likely to lose one of the sections in my wicked tailgate. The drawback is cost. A "travel rod" costs a little more. However, if you're going to do a lot of packing or traveling, it's worth considering.

Where Not to Cut Corners. Buy the most expensive rod you can realistically afford. You can cut a lot of corners in fly casting, and I'll do my best to show you where, but rod selection is not the place to do it. Along with your fly line, it's the sport's lifeblood.

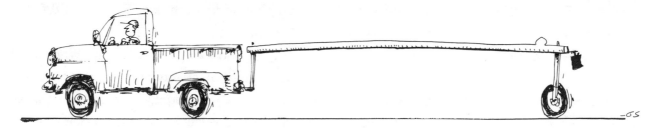

CARRYING CASE/TRAILER FOR SINGLE-PIECE RODS

If you can afford only a cheap rod, instead of the one you want, my recommendation is to wait—or to use the money you would have spent on a cheap rod as a down payment or a layaway. It pains me to say this, but, in rods, cheap is just a waste of your money.

Rods are not all equal. But if you look around, you can find one that will fit your budget, needs, and personal tastes. My advice is to avoid glass rods and cheap graphite models entirely. Don't settle for less than the bottom end of the "okay" rods.

A good rod will grow with you and last a long time, but expect to pay over $100. A *really* good rod will cost $300 to $400. An entry-level rod, workable but not brilliant, will set you back around $50. If you want to have your fly casting cake and eat it too, consider a very good entry-level setup, like Sage's Discovery. It's a fine rod that will give you plenty of fishing enjoyment for under $150. Many top-notch rod makers, and Sage is a leader, would like to sell you one of their best rods. However, rod builders know you may not be ready for a state-of-the-art rod with a state-of-the-art price tag. Still, you want a first-rate piece of equipment. The Discovery fills the bill. It uses a Graphite II (IM-6) blank, which translates into higher line speed and more distance. For a lot less money (and less performance), the Browning Diana is a good outfit. However, you will outgrow it sooner.

Safes for Fly Rods and Reels. In Oregon, I grew up in the country. I never remember locking a door. But that was a different time, and things have changed.

After you fish for a while, you might find yourself needing several good rods and upgrades on fly reels. This amounts to a lifetime investment. It runs into money, and equipment can be hard to replace. One good rod costs as much as a good shotgun, yet expensive gear is often carelessly left lying about. A thief who breaks into your home can carry off thousands of dollars' worth of gear, and you've made it easy for him if you leave your stuff in plain sight.

When you aren't fishing, put those rods and reels up. A safe for firearms makes a good storage place. There's a growing demand for hot, quality fishing gear. A fly rod is easy to fence, and lots of people will buy it without asking questions. In addition to locking up firearms, cameras, bonds, and jewelry, it's a must to secure your rods and reels. If you don't have a safe, at least hide your gear in an obscure place, so the thief will have to work for his booty.

The Least You Should Know About Fly Lines

Huck Finn had the right idea. As Miss Watson was cramming religion and civilization down his throat, she told Huck he could pray for anything he wanted. Naturally, he prayed about fishing. Huck was pleased to get a fishing line—he knew the value of a good line. He was a little disappointed, nonetheless, that God didn't give him some hooks to go with it, so he quit believing.

It's always a good idea to pray about fishing. Nowadays, though, asking for a line isn't enough. It's more complicated than that.

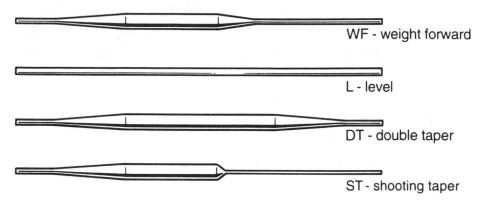

WF - weight forward

L - level

DT - double taper

ST - shooting taper

Fly lines.

You need to know what type of fishing you'll be doing and what conditions you'll be facing, so you can pray for the right line.

By now you know that all lines are not the same. Like rods, some lines are so cheap that they are a waste of money. Lines also have different uses. They come in various sizes, grades, functions, and weights. For example, a #4 line is lighter than a #8 line. As I mentioned earlier, a #5, #6, or #7 line is a good all-around choice for many fly casters.

Let's talk about what else you should know about lines. When we say the weight of a line, we are referring to how many grams the first 30 feet of line will weigh. Thus, the first 30 feet of a #3 would weigh three grams, the same length of a #8 line would weigh eight grams.

You probably have an idea about what line weight you want to use, but let's clear the water. When you walk into a tackle store or a fishing shop and look at lines, you're likely to get pretty damn confused. Besides lines theoretically ranging from #1 to #13, you'll find a host of trendy colors from white to blaze orange to chartreuse. Add to this varying tapers,

densities, and prices. It was a lot easier in the days of spin casting, but never fear. Boxes of fly line list the important things you need to know—information about *taper, line weight,* and *function.* For example, a box of line might read as follows: *WF-6-F.* It might seem confusing, but it actually makes sense. Next we'll look at line labeling in more detail.

Taper in Fly Lines. As you know, your fly line helps determine the size of fish you'll cast for and the size of fly you'll use. But let's get more specific about tapers. A fly line, especially the first 25 to 35 feet, is formed into various shapes that are designed for different functions. Here's an overview:

Weight Forward	**WF**
Weight Forward (bass, salt)	**WR**
Level	**L**
Double Taper	**DT**
Shooting Taper	**ST**

Weight Forward Taper Line. As you would expect, the weight is consolidated in the first 30 feet or so, making it the easiest line to cast.

The rest of the line is narrower and lighter, so it will zip through the guides. Since tapered lines are easy to cast, they are a good choice for beginners as well as expert fly casters. A WF line is my favorite. A little casting delicacy may be lost with a WF line, but I think it's worth the compromise.

Weight Forward Taper (Bass/Salt Line). These lines (sometimes called bug or salt tapers) are designed along the same lines as a regular WF line, but even more weight is concentrated toward the front. A bass taper is a long caster that will buck the wind. When you're using a bass bug fly or fishing on salt water, it has decided advantages. A soft, ethereal cast is not one of them.

Level Taper Line. This line will hurt your wallet the least. However, it will also be a mediocre line at best. As the name implies, it has the same diameter from end to end, without a taper. Since there's no taper, it's virtually impossible to get a dainty presentation or distance.

Double Taper Line. This line is really two lines for the price of one, and it's probably the best value for the fly caster. You can cast a long way, and cast well, with a double taper line. It is *the* taper for all-around fishing. Each end of the line is tapered, giving you a graceful cast and a soft presentation. When you wear out one side, you simply reverse the ends. The DT is initially a little more expensive, but it's an excellent choice for your first line. You'll soon be casting like a pro.

Shooting Taper Line. This is a distinctive, specialized taper, sometimes referred to as a shooting head line. It allows you to *shoot* your line across the water. This line might be used by a salmon, steelhead, or bass fly caster who needs to get the line way out there. Those who are looking for 80- to 100-foot casts find this system useful. The weight of the line is centered heavily in the front section, while the rest of the line (the running line) is of smaller diameter, so it follows quickly. This is an advanced, specialized line, so you'll want to cast for a while before you worry about a shooting line.

For your purposes at this point, I would recommend either the double taper line or the weight forward line. I think the WF feels a little better, but the DT might be a better value because you'll be getting that second line. You will be practicing a lot at first, so your line will wear out rapidly. After you've taken the rough edges off your casting by practicing in your yard, you can reverse your DT line and have a brand new one to work with.

If you start with a WF, you will need to replace it before long. However, because of the construction of the line, you will learn casting quickly. Then, for your second line, you can purchase one that's more expensive.

In any case, your first line should be a good, middle-of-the-road line. Avoid low-end lines.

How Line Weight Functions. The second designation on that labeled box of line ("6") indicates the weight of the line. Back in the fly casting dark ages, lines were differentiated by their diameters, so they could be balanced to a specific rod. Diameters and weights were not uniform, so letters were employed to symbolize different sizes. It was very complicated, and I get a headache thinking about it. The perception that lines are complicated has lingered, but it's much easier to set yourself up now. You used to have to be a rocket scientist. Now the guesswork has mostly been eliminated.

From our discussion earlier in the chapter, you know that a #5, #6, or #7 rod/line combination is a good place to start. These weights are general enough to handle a broad spectrum of fishing styles, demands, and species, yet focused enough to be enjoyable.

Lines up to #4 are designed for calm, clear spring creeks where the fish have graduate degrees in recognizing the differences between your fly and the real thing. You have to make a perfect, snowy presentation with a fly so small you can hardly see it, and your leader must be hair-thin. When you do get a fish, you run a 60 percent chance of breaking the leader when you lift to set the hook. It's an awfully fun kind of fishing, but it's specialized.

Lines #5 to #7 are good all-around weights. Your best choice will depend on what and where you fish. If you go with a good graphite rod, parting with a share of the family food budget for the month, you can buy a lightweight rod and still cast a heavy line if necessary. Consider the wind in your area, and whether you're going to fish wet flies or streamers (large wet flies). If there's not much wind and you'll be using dry flies to achieve a delicate presentation, go small. If you'll use streamers, fish wet, or face significant wind, go heavy.

Lines #8 and up are for heavy waters and big fish like salmon and steelhead. They're useful if you'll be contending with lots of wind.

How Line Functions. How does your fly line work? What does it do? Different lines do different things for different types of fishing. The third part of that labeled box of line ("F") tells you how the line functions. There are several general categories:

Floating Line	**F**
Sinking Line	**S**
Floating with Sink Tip	**F/S**

Floating Line. As the name implies, this is a line that floats on the water, and it's the one most commonly used by line fly casters. In fly casting's dark ages, lines were made of silk. To keep the line afloat, a fly fisher had to apply floatant all over the line. When the fishing was done, the line was hung out to dry, or it would go sour and rot. Today, thankfully, our lines are made of plastic, and are practically maintenance-free. It doesn't hurt to rinse out a line once in a while, but that's about all you have to do. When modern lines are manufactured, air bubbles are forced into the plastic, making them buoyant to a greater or lesser degree. A floating line is your best—and probably your only—bet for a first line. You can fish dry flies with it, but you can also weight the leader and fish wet.

Sinking Line. This line will sink from one end to the other. However, sinking lines sink at different speeds. Depending on the type of water you're fishing, you may want a line to sink quickly or slowly. For most fly fishers, a medium sink line is the best choice. You'll probably want to invest in sinking lines later, when you're fishing waters where you want to get your fly deep.

Floating with Sink Tip. With these lines, the body of the line floats, the tip sinks. If the first part of the line sinks—up to the first ten feet—it's a *sink tip line.* If 20 feet or so sinks (past the taper), it's a *sink taper line.* If the first thirty feet or more sinks, it's a *sinking belly line.* For certain types of specialized fishing, it's handy to have a portion of the line float while the rest sinks, so you can get your fly down to intermediate depths.

Get a Good Line. Don't cut corners on line. It's what carries your fly. Generally, you should buy the best line you can afford. As I mentioned earlier, however, you will wear a line out in the first few months if you practice much. For your first line, go with a good quality and replace it when it gets rough. When you pick up more skill, you'll learn to appreciate a better line. Go for the best when it matters. Ultimately, saving $5 or $10 by going with a cheaper line is no

bargain. You can't skimp on line or rods, because they're critically important pieces of equipment.

Color of the Line. There are a zillion colors. What color turns you on?

I'm not sure color matters. Some think that brighter lines scare fish, or that shadows from brighter lines scare fish. There might be something to this, but I haven't noticed it.

I like a bright color because I can see it better and thus control it—in the air as well as on the water. A bright color is especially helpful when you're learning to cast, because you can easily see it. If all else fails, get a color to match your eyes.

Backing Your Fly Line. Every once in a while, you'll get a good fish that will spool all your fly line. You'll pray for these times. At moments like this, you're glad you have backing on your reel. Every fly line should be backed with a 15- to 30-pound test Dacron line.

When you wind your fly line, you'll notice there's leftover space on the reel. This was done

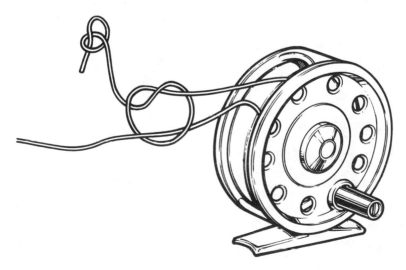

Attaching the backing to the reel is as simple as two granny knots.

***Your reel is a good place
to store plenty of line.***

on purpose so you could add backing, thus filling up the reel. But you don't want to overload. To get the proper balance:

1. Wind your fly line (taper first) onto the reel.
2. Wind on the backing until it *starts* to fill the spool. Don't overload.
3. Unwind the backing and the fly line.
4. Tie the backing to the spool using two granny knots. Wind on the backing. Tie the backing to the fly line.
5. When you're done, the reel should not be overloaded. If it is, strip off the line and remove a few yards of backing.

The Least You Should Know About Reels

If you have to cut corners, do it on your reel.

Most of the time, a reel is no more than a fine place to store fly line. For me, at least, a reel isn't a fashion statement. If you're after large fish, maybe an expensive reel is in order, but a cheap reel will serve you well. You can upgrade later, as circumstances permit.

I've never owned a really expensive reel. For years I used *el cheapo* reels and caught plenty of fish. I've since found that intermediate models are good buys. I've upgraded to Scientific Anglers System I (a really good, moderately priced click-drag) and System II (disc-drag) reels. I'd rather use my extra dollars to upgrade my rods or line.

There are three types of reels:

Automatic reels, spring-loaded, are rarely used by serious fly casters. They don't work well, and they break easily. I don't know anyone who uses one.

A *single-action (click-drag)* reel is a spool with a grip. This is the reel most fly casters use. A revolution of the handle is a revolution of the spool. A simple reel of this nature is not heavy, and it's usually problem-free. The pawl-click-drag is good for most fishing waters. This reel gives only one or two points of drag around the reel—on a fast run with a big fish, it will wobble. It's a simple design that has worked for years. A good single-action reel will run from $15 to $80.

A *multiple gear (disc-drag)* reel is a little more complicated and a lot smoother. As the name implies, it has gears. The drags are true disc-drags. They make large fish easier to land, since the drag is smoother and more uniform. It's less likely to wobble, because the spool tightens down evenly and counter-balances itself. A disc-drag reel will start at just over $50 and climb dramatically. A middle-of-the-road model might cost just under $200. Custom reels of this nature are very nice, very light, very smooth, and very expensive. For most of us, owning one would be like storing a 1975 VW Super Beetle in a million-dollar garage. In other words, it's a luxury you probably don't need.

A good single action reel will serve you well. I've used a Scientific Anglers System I click-drag reel for years. It has a strong frame, an adjustable click-drag, an exposed rim, and a counterbalanced spool. A little more care must be taken when landing big fish, but I've enjoyed the challenge, and I haven't burned up the reel yet. I don't use the drag that much on small fish. I'm impressed by the System II reel, also. It's a fish-stopper, and it may be the most popular disc fly reel in the world. The drag adjusts from one to seven pounds, and the brake pads will hold up to the heat. This reel has a widely

exposed spool for palming, and it holds plenty of backing.

Always fish with your drag on the lowest setting, so you don't break your leader. Get into the habit of checking. If you need more drag, *palm the spool.* (Run your palm or finger over the exposed bottom portion of the spool as the fish is taking out line.)

Another advantage to having an exposed rim is the ability to change spools. If you can purchase an extra spool with your reel, do it. An extra spool is handy, if only to hold your old line for yard practice. With the right reel, you can switch spools quickly.

Not all reels, however, have exposed spools. Don't buy one that doesn't. If there's a casing around it, don't get it.

The Least You Should Know About Leader

The key word on leader is *tapered.* The thinnest part, the tippet, is tied to your fly. The thickest part, the butt, is tied to your fly line. Your leader separates the fly from the fly line. It's supposed to provide enough distance so the fish will not associate your fly presentation with fly line. The line is tapered to add a final touch to your cast, so you can accurately hit your target. The acceleration or power of the cast is translated from the fly line to your leader. The leader lays over (turns over when cast) with the fly, setting down on the water in a calm, snowflake-like manner.

You can tie your own leader; in fact, it's the traditional thing to do. But for now, it's a lot

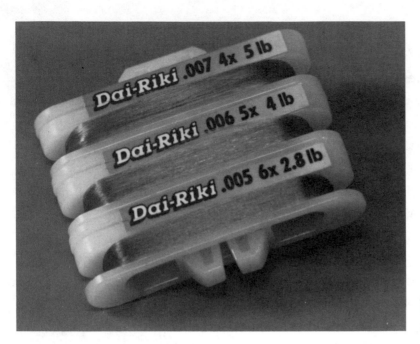

A leader caddy like this one is a handy way to carry extra tippet material.

easier to buy them. They are chemically tapered, which produces a smooth presentation, and you won't have to worry about knots coming undone or collecting moss. I tie my own only if I'm in the backwoods and my last store-bought leader is history.

Buy two or three 9-foot leaders. It's good to have a backup. If you need to shorten one down to make a 7 1/2 –foot leader, simply cut a couple of feet off.

Leaders wear down, as you'd suspect, since you tie on flies. The bottom part will naturally be clipped up as you tie. Rather than tying on another leader when you've used it up, keep a few spools of 2-, 4-, and 6-pound-test line on hand and tie it to the leader to replenish. You can also make a more delicate presentation for your fly, if need be, by adding a lighter tippet, thus increasing the length.

There are a lot of diameter considerations in fly leader, and it gives me a headache when I start to think about them. I'm not sure I've

ever really understood line diameter, but neither have the fish I've caught.

For the record, in case it's really important, the butt of the leader (the part you attach to your fly line) should be about two-thirds the diameter of the end of your fly line. The idea is to continue the gradual taper.

When you buy leader it will come in 1X, 2X, 3X . . . 6X, 7X, and so on. The front of the package will usually break down the vital statistics. What you need to worry about is the length of the leader and the pound-test break point. As an example, the front of the leader package might say:

Knotless Tapered Leader
9 ft 5X 4 lb

This tells us that the leader is 9 feet long and has a 4-pound-test tippet, or end. This would make it a 5X leader.

Buy a quality leader. A cheap leader is stiff and has too much memory. It will turn brittle in the sun and kink up. You'll save a few pen-

Leader	Lb-Test	Butt Diameter	Tip Diameter
1X	12 lbs	.023 butt	.010 tip
2X	10 lbs	.023 butt	.009 tip
3X	7 lbs	.023 butt	.008 tip
4X	5 lbs	.023 butt	.007 tip
5X	4 lbs	.023 butt	.006 tip
6X	2.5 lbs	.023 butt	.005 tip
7X	1.8 lbs	.023 butt	.004 tip

Many leader packages include a chart like this one, so you can check the leader size.

nies, but it will cost you a few dollars' worth of frustration. Maybe a fish, too. You can't go wrong with any of the following brands: Dai-Riki, Umpqua, Scientific Anglers, Cortland. My observations about these lines are as follows:

Dai-Riki: High knot strength and low memory. The stiffness is good for turning over heavy flies, but not as subtle on the most delicate presentations. This is my favorite leader.

Umpqua: A little more flexible and has good knot strength. Very good for delicate presentations. A thin diameter per pound-test.

Scientific Anglers: A little stiff. Throws big, weighted flies comfortably and is very resistant to abrasions.

Cortland: Very subtle, high knot strength, a little thinner diameter per actual pound-test. Good color.

How to Get to the Fish

You have to get near enough to the fish so you can cast productively. You might stand on the bank in some situations; in others, you can fish from a boat or a canoe or you can wade. Most fly casters wade, because it's often the best way to approach fish without spooking them. It's also the best way to get close enough to cast (and get away from the bank, so your back cast doesn't catch bushes). You don't need waders if the water is warm and shallow, or if you have room to cast from the bank. But this situation is often hard to come by. Waders make wading comfortable. More often than not, if you want to catch fish, you'll need to use them.

A package of tapered leader.

A wader/boot case like this one makes transporting your wet waders and boots a cinch.

Waders are an essential piece of equipment if you'll be fishing in cold water or cold weather.

I must confess that I never owned a set of waders until I was 19 years old. I could have used them, but I was just too stupid and broke to know that I needed them. I jumped into the icy streams of southern Oregon like there was no tomorrow, plunging ahead while wet from the waist down. Wearing either Levis or shorts, I'd wade and cast until I was blue. During the summer, I didn't seem to mind. In the spring and autumn, I couldn't always fish as long as I'd like. I was a lot tougher then, but I'm smarter now. When I got waders for my nineteenth birthday, I wondered how I ever got along without them. Fly casting became much more comfortable.

Waders come in two styles: hip waders and chest waders. Hip waders are useful when you're trudging through the Alaskan bush and swampy areas, or when fishing small streams that aren't too deep. For deep water and float tubes (one-person rafts that look something like glorified inner tubes), chest waders are the order of the day. Chest waders are usually the better choice unless you're fishing spring creeks and small streams.

Waders are made from neoprene of some sort, or from rubber (or a rubber combination). Neoprene waders are preferred by many fly casters. They create less drag, because they fit snugly, like a loose wet suit. They're also warmer. Neoprene waders are a little more expensive, but they last a lot longer and they don't crack. If they do need repairs, they're easy to fix. You can buy different thicknesses of neoprene, and your need will vary depending on how early or late in the season you intend to fish and how cold the water will be.

Cheap rubber waders will last a season or two. Or you can spend about double the price and get a good set. They create more drag than neoprene waders do when you're in the current or kicking in a float tube, but even a cheap set of rubber waders will serve you.

Some waders have a built-in shoe or boot. Others don't, and these are called stocking waders. Most neoprene outfits are stocking waders, but you can buy a boot to go with them. If you do much walking, a stocking wader and boot will be more comfortable. You get better support, and you're more secure when you're walking over slippery rocks in the water.

When it comes to wading boots, I strongly recommend buying a boot with a felt sole. The felt sole will give you sure footing on slippery rocks. If you've ever waded without felt soles, or had a broken leg because you slipped, you'll know they are well worth it. If you buy a cheap set of rubber waders with a conventional sole, you can glue carpet or felt on the bottoms and get satisfactory results.

Wear a belt around your waist outside the waders, especially with rubber waders. The belt ensures that, if you take a tumble, your waders won't fill up with water. You'll get wet, but you'll retain a buoyant air pocket.

Tools and Where to Put Them

When you're fishing, you'll need to carry some essential tools around. The longer you cast, the more essentials you'll think you need. I'm sometimes hunched over as a result of my gear,

These are stocking foot waders that are worn inside of sneakers or wading boots.

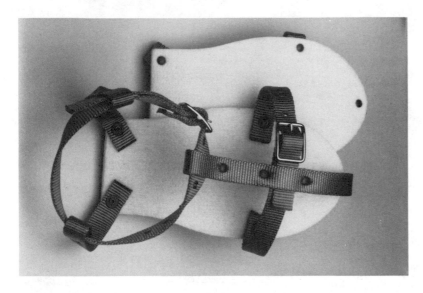

Buckle-on felt pads make you more sure-footed when you're wearing rubber-soled waders.

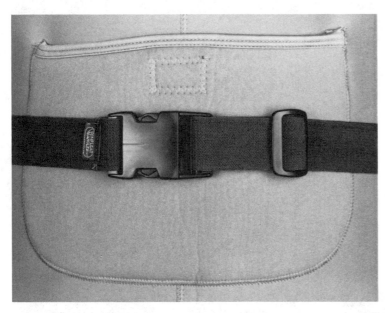

A wading belt is critical if you fish with rubber waders, because the waders would otherwise fill with water if you accidentally took a swim. The belt could even save your life.

Fly boxes keep your flies portable and organized.

even though I constantly strive to simplify. At the very least, you'll need to carry a few basics:

- Tapered leaders
- A few spools of leader
- Hemostat or long needle-nose pliers (for removing a hook from a fish's mouth)
- Nail clippers, tied on a rope that dangles from vest or pack (to clip line)
- A small box of assorted lead shot
- Floating solvent (like Gink or Nev-R-Sink)
- Fly boxes for wet and dry flies (write your name and address on them)
- Strike indicators
- Polarized glasses

Here are a few things you might want to collect a little later:

- Thermometer (for checking the temperature of the water)
- Net
- Stomach pump (to see what the fish has eaten)
- Bug screen
- Scissors (to trim flies or remove wings)
- Small field glasses (to look for bug activity)
- Pepper spray (when in bear country)
- Swiss Army knife (or something like it). These knives have a million tools, and you can do most anything with them—from gutting a fish to fixing a reel, starting a fire (with magnifying lens), and clipping flies or line (with the scissors). This is the best knife on the market, and you'll wonder how you ever got along without it.
- Insect repellent, sunscreen, lunch, etc.

You need something to put your equipment in. When you first start, you might get along with a fly box stuffed in your pocket, but it doesn't take long to collect more than you can possibly carry in the pockets of your jeans. At one time, a fly vest was the perfect solution. Now, in addition to a vest, you might select a fanny pack, a chest pack, or a backpack specially made for fly casting.

I've used a vest for years. They're handy if you aren't carrying a ton of gear. When I go heavy, I really enjoy the new chest packs, fanny packs, or combinations thereof.

You'll want to select a "carrying" system that suits your needs. There's a selection available in every price range. Don't part with your hard-earned bucks too soon, though. Fish for a while, talk to others, then decide what you want. Don't buy an expensive carrying system until you know what you want to carry.

A good pair of polarized sunglasses will help you see past the glare and into the water, making it easier to keep track of your fly and to see a fish rise.

*Whether you're casting wet or dry, a good cast is
one of the most delightful aspects of fly fishing.*

FOUR

Sermon on the Cast
The Essence of Casting upon Water

THIS CHAPTER WILL DESCRIBE THE BASIC TECHNIQUES NEEDED TO EFFECTIVELY CAST A FLY. We will look at casting styles and what to do in different fishing situations. You'll be ready to fish after half an hour's practice on the front lawn. And no matter what anyone says, you *can* catch fish. You have a way to go, but you're getting there.

The Compleat Concept of Practice

I wasn't lying. After half an hour's practice, you're ready for the water. You won't be casting perfectly, but you'll be putting your practice to use. And you'll be hooking a few fish, too. Being on the water gives you the big picture. It puts the pieces together. You're here to fish, not just to cast perfect lines on manicured lawns in order to impress your jealous neighbors. Being a fly caster does create all sorts of envy, though.

Getting on the water will help you understand what you need to work on, but practice time isn't over yet. Lots of casting makes perfect, as the cliché goes. In addition to regular fishing intervals (as frequently as you can manage them) plan to work on your cast on a regular basis for at least two weeks. Better make it four weeks.

Consistent, frequent casting practice will cement what you're learning. Casting may be an art, but it's a motor skill first—a skill that can only be learned the old-fashioned way. A regular workout will do wonders for your loops. If you practice for a month, 5 to 15 minutes at a time and maybe four times a week, you'll be casting like an old hand. A month's consistent work will make you look like you've been at it for years. Combine this with a few all-day fishing trips, and you have the battle half won.

I still keep a loaded fly rod in my garage. Several times a week, I'll go out and work on some element of my cast. Fly fishing is a continual progression. You get to one plateau and there's another one on the horizon. Then another.

For the record, five minutes of daily practice will yield better results than a long marathon session on Saturday. Yard practice is like drills and scrimmages for a ballplayer. If one good session a week was the best way to train, ball clubs would have an all-day practice once a week and leave it at that. Realistically, though, a long practice on Saturday is a whole lot better than nothing. Not all of us can throw line every day in the front yard. There are braces to be bought, mortgages to be met, and expensive pieces of fly gear to be purchased. My advice is to cast as often as you can. The more you work at it, the more you'll progress.

In any case, remember that you're here to have fun. This is a lifetime sport, and you have the rest of your days to work at it.

Frustration Levels. Some casters want to be perfect overnight. For most of us, it just doesn't happen that way. But don't worry, you probably can't walk on water, either. You'll have to wade. Your line is going to pile at your feet. You'll hook your ear. You'll slap the water. Worse, you'll be fishing near someone who can really cast, and you'll feel self-conscious. Don't get down on yourself. Everyone who's made it out of fly casting boot camp has had similar feelings. It takes a certain amount of frustration to realize all the joy you'll so richly deserve after a month or so of practice. If it helps, when you're casting around the pros and you feel like the village idiot, do what they tell nervous public speakers to do. Imagine that the members of the audience (in your case, the other casters) are in their underwear. Then you won't feel so bad. Imagine how cold that water must feel on their bare legs!

Be gentle on yourself. If you think some pro is staring at you, say, "I guess you can tell I'm still learning. Any pointers will be appreciated." Most casters will pass on a useful comment or two. Sure, the other guy is a snob, but

you can bet he remembers what it's like to look the way you do now. More than likely, he or she is proud of you for trying and will be happy to give you a few hints. Snobbery is really a thin veneer. You can get past it quickly.

You're now in the big leagues. Remember this Rutter Postulate: It's better to be the world's worst fly fisher than the world's best Power Bait user. Or if that's not good enough, remember that you're smarter than more than ten million worm fishermen whose idea of a good time is catching a dense, put-and-take rainbow!

See? You're already on your way to snobdom.

But back to casting. Accuracy over distance is the key to good casting. Getting your line out there a long way is useful—at times it's the only way to get some fish—but *how* and *where* you place your line is more important. The old golf adage, "You drive for show and putt for dough," can be reworded to form another Rutter Postulate: You cast long for show and accurately for fish.

Cast to an old milk jug 25 or 30 feet away. Later, you'll catch a lot of fish at this distance. As you get good at dropping your fly on the jug, push it out five or ten feet farther. It's foolish to try to cast 50 or 60 feet when you haven't mastered accuracy at shorter distances, so be patient.

Basic Casting Principles

I know you're eager to pick up the rod. I'm the same way. You may have already fooled around casting in the yard. Either way, there are some guiding principles you'll want to keep in mind. Let's grab your rod and reel. You don't need to fully assemble the rod (if you're in your house or office, it might not be practical). Just the reel and the bottom (or butt) section of the rod will do for now.

The 11:00 to 1:00 cast.

Right: *Practice taking your rod through the three major positions—12:00, 11:00, and 1:00. Start with the rod straight up and your elbow tucked in to your side.*

Below left: *Keeping your elbow centered, move your arm and rod back to 1:00 in one fluid motion.*

Below right: *Move your arm and rod forward to 11:00, keeping your elbow as stationary as possible.*

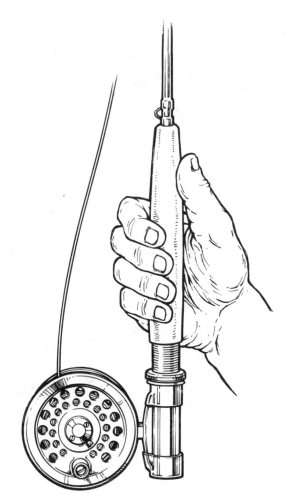

The grip. Grasp the handle firmly, with your thumb pointing toward the tip of the rod.

The Grip. With the reel facing down, grip the rod snugly halfway up the cork, with your thumb pointing up the rod. Later, you can move your thumb or use your index finger to point up the rod, but for now use your thumb as I've suggested. Once you've learned the basics, then it's okay to break the rules.

Theory has it that your thumb keeps your arm straight. As we'll learn in a moment, you'll be bringing your arm straight back, parallel to your body.

In my opinion, a traditional casting stance is highly overrated. When you're actually fishing, you're standing and casting every which way. For lawn casting, and for your first few times out, stand directly in front of where you want to cast. Now turn about six to eight inches (30 degrees) to the right if you are right-handed, or to the left if you are left-handed.

The 30-degree turn allows you to look at your back cast. For a while, you'll want to glance over your shoulder, so you can see if your line is straight.

There's little breaking of your wrist. It isn't exactly locked in place, but remember to keep it in about the same position throughout your cast.

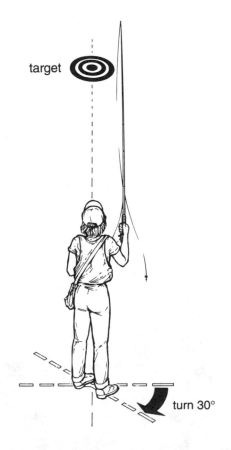

target

turn 30°

The practice stance. You want to be able to see the line while back casting.
1. *Face the target.*
2. *Turn 30° toward your casting arm.*
3. *When you back cast, look over your shoulder at the line. Don't start the forward cast until the line lies flat behind you.*
4. *Aim your fly for the target.*

When you practice casting, pretend you're standing in front of a large clock. During the cast, your rod tip passes from 11:00 to 1:00 and from 1:00 to 11:00.

The 11:00 to 1:00 Cast. Casting is a smooth, fluid motion . . . okay, not at first. It's awkward. Never forget that the weight of the line casts your fly. Let's work through the motions.

Keep in mind that wherever your rod tip goes, your line must follow. When you cast you will use the 11:00 to 1:00 method. Imagine a large clock at your side—on your right side if you're right-handed, on your left side if you're left-handed—while you are casting. The tip of your rod will go from 11:00 to 1:00. You'll pause for roughly one to two seconds while the line straightens out from the rod tip (so it's parallel

to the ground), then you'll move the rod back again to 11:00.

Practice without line, using the imaginary clock. No jerking. It's a pull and push motion. Or rather, it's:

1) Start at 11:00 and pull until 12:00 . . . then accelerate until 1:00 . . . then pause!
2) Start at 1:00 and push until 12:00 . . . then accelerate until 11:00 . . . then pause!

Let's examine this in more detail. Hold your rod at 11:00. Pull the rod straight back, with your elbow remaining in roughly the same position. At about 12:00, accelerate until 1:00 and hold. The length of the pause will eventually depend on how much line you have out.

Now push forward from the 1:00 position. Remember that the line should flatten out before you pull, which is why you are turned so you can see over your shoulder. At 12:00, accelerate until you get to 11:00. You've got the basic motions down (push/pull, accelerate, pause).

What Are Loops? After you master the basic movements, it's time to add one more element to make your cast complete—the wrist snap. This will help you control your loops. When I talk about a *loop*, I mean the candy-cane shape your fly line assumes when you're doing a forward or backward cast.

Most of the time, you'll want a tight loop. At the least, you need to know how to throw a tight line with a loop from two to four feet wide at the "J." A tight loop is energy efficient, because it creates a fast cast that cuts through the air and bucks the wind. A tight loop is a must for long, accurate casts. Besides, a tight loop also looks nice and adds to your snob appeal. If a pilot is judged by the smoothness of the landing, a fly caster is often judged by the tightness of the loops.

A tight loop is harder to master than a wide loop. When you're throwing tight loops, you must snap your wrist momentarily at the end

WHAT DO WE MEAN BY
LINE LOOPS?

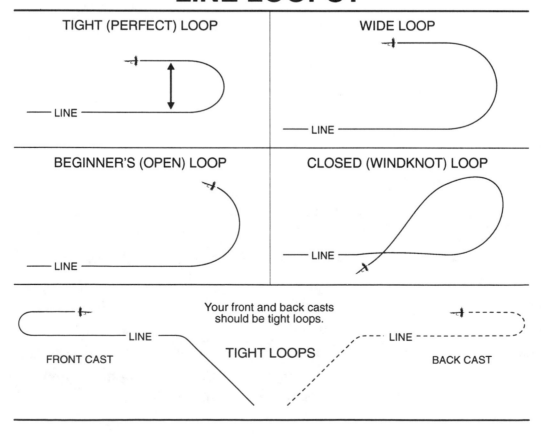

TIGHT (PERFECT) LOOP

WIDE LOOP

LINE

LINE

BEGINNER'S (OPEN) LOOP

CLOSED (WINDKNOT) LOOP

LINE

LINE

Your front and back casts should be tight loops.

LINE

TIGHT LOOPS

LINE

FRONT CAST

BACK CAST

HOW TO GET TIGHT LOOPS

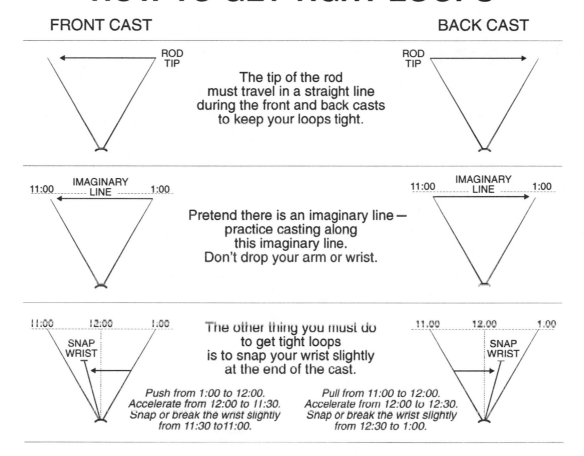

FRONT CAST

BACK CAST

The tip of the rod must travel in a straight line during the front and back casts to keep your loops tight.

Pretend there is an imaginary line — practice casting along this imaginary line. Don't drop your arm or wrist.

The other thing you must do to get tight loops is to snap your wrist slightly at the end of the cast.

Push from 1:00 to 12:00. Accelerate from 12:00 to 11:30. Snap or break the wrist slightly from 11:30 to 11:00.

Pull from 11:00 to 12:00. Accelerate from 12:00 to 12:30. Snap or break the wrist slightly from 12:30 to 1:00.

of your delivery. Wide loops, from four to seven feet wide at the "J," mean a slow cast. They're often associated with wet casting. Wide loops allow you to throw bigger flies or throw weight (metal shot) on the line. A slow cast and a wide loop is necessary in some situations because you want the fly or leaded line to drop quickly. The width of the loop keeps the heavy fly or lead from tangling and crossing up during the cast, because it has farther to drop. A wide line is easier to throw, because it's slower and you keep your wrist locked. There's no snap.

Getting a tight loop when you cast is an orchestrated effort. You need to do two things:

1. Make sure your rod tip travels in a straight line (from 11:00 to 1:00 or 1:00 to 11:00).

2. Snap your wrist slightly forward at the end of your front cast and slightly backward at the end of your back cast. This supercharges the acceleration on the line, keeping the loops tight and controlled.

The faster you snap your wrist, the tighter loop you'll throw. It might seem a little awkward at first, but you'll get the hang of it with practice. There are two things I would caution you about—pitfalls that snag casters who aren't aware.

1. Don't drop your elbow or arm during the cast.
2. Don't get into the habit of holding your arm in one place and snapping or flicking your wrist. Only snap your wrist at the prescribed times—during the front cast from 11:30 to 11:00 or during the back cast from 12:30 to 1:00.

Dropping your arm causes all sorts of problems. The rod must travel on an even plane. In the old days when you learned how to fly cast, you pinned a book against your side and held it there with your elbow. During the casting process, the book was never supposed to drop. This regimentation forced the caster to keep his or her casting smooth, preventing the elbow (or the arm or shoulder) from dropping. Most modern casters don't keep their elbows snug against their sides like the traditional English caster might. However, if you find yourself dropping your arm or elbow, it might help

you in the short run to try the old book trick. Remember that your line follows your rod tip—your line does whatever your rod tip tells it to do. If you drop your arm, you drop your rod, and your line whips about accordingly. If you are getting an erratic line, work on keeping the rod even.

Watch getting too "wristy." It's a bad habit to get into. Use the orchestrated approach we've discussed. On short casts, you'll see some casters use their wrists, but don't do it. Not yet. Wait until you've mastered your cast first. Relying on your wrist can lead to a

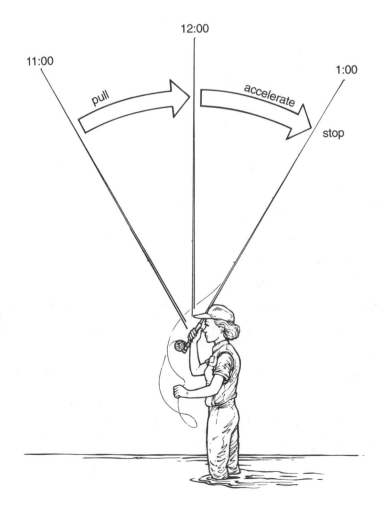

The back cast.

lot of problems unless you've got the funda-mentals down.

The correct casting motion goes like this: For a *back cast*, you smartly pull the rod back from 11:00 to 12:00. At 12:00 you accelerate your cast. At 12:30 you continue the acceleration but you snap your wrist backward slightly until the rod tip gets to 1:00, where you pause.

For a *front cast*, you smartly push the rod forward from 1:00 to 12:00. At 12:00, you accelerate your cast. At 11:30 you continue the acceleration but you snap your wrist forward slightly until the rod tip gets to 11:00, where you stop.

You have just gone through the basic cast. When your rod is fully assembled, you will notice a more whipping motion, and actual "clock" distance may tighten up since it's the tip of the rod that goes from 11:00 to 1:00. But you will adjust quickly. You'll also notice the bend in your rod when you're casting. This bend is what powers your line.

As a point of interest, I've noticed that many women take to fly casting more easily than men do, because they don't overpower. Macho force is not the way to arrive at a good cast. Try for a solid, fluid motion. The move-

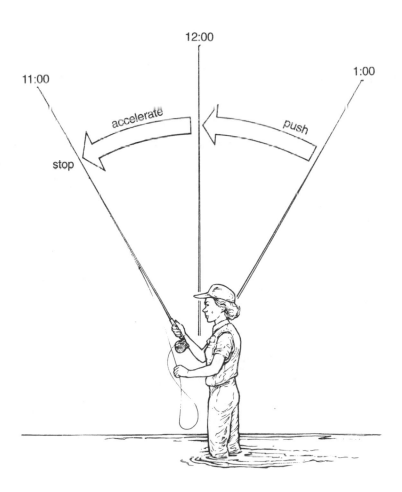

The forward cast.

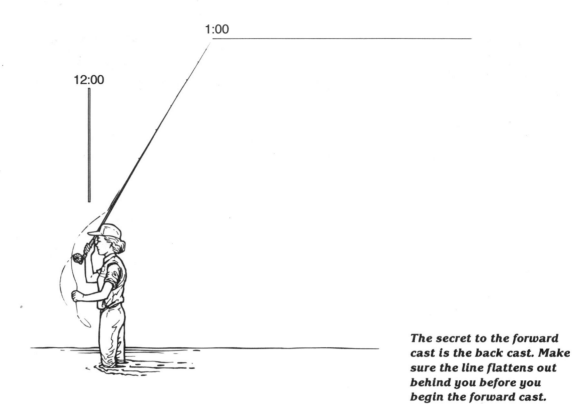

The secret to the forward cast is the back cast. Make sure the line flattens out behind you before you begin the forward cast.

ment of your arm, the snap of the wrist, and the natural flexibility of your rod will do your work, not your muscles. Your arm shouldn't be sore after a day of fishing. If it is, you're overpowering. Casting is a matter of finesse, not force.

Remember Your Back Cast. Most novice casters seem to encounter several problems, all dealing with the back cast. I'll repeat this later, but I want you to think about your back cast now, before you actually start. The back cast is the secret to your front cast . . . in fact, it's the secret to accuracy. Master the back cast and you've mastered fly fishing. Here are Rutter's not-so-original tips for success:

- Don't pull the rod back too far. There's a temptation to think that if 1:00 is good, then 3:00 is better. It ain't.

- Let your line flatten out behind you before starting the forward cast.
- Don't overpower the forward cast. This isn't a game of tennis. Our culture and our preoccupation with sports seem to naturally condition us toward a powerful forward move that's not needed in fly fishing. Conversely, we are inclined to have a wimpy back cast. Here's where most of us could apply a little more power, especially when we're lifting the line off the water or the lawn.

The Line. Your line's the key to everything. Keep it under control.

You can see your forward cast, so it's easy to control. The back cast is the bug in the ointment. After you pull back, you must not push forward until your line is laid out behind you. It sounds easy, but it takes some practice. It's what sets up your delivery. A proper back cast is the most important thing you can remember. If you pull forward too soon, before the "J" loop has flattened out, you'll lose control of your line in varying degrees, you'll snap off the fly, you'll create wind knots, your fly will slap the water, the line will pile up, a fly will hook your ear, or you'll lose accuracy.

Casting on the Lawn

Here's where you put it all together. If you don't have a lawn, find a grassy area like a park.

For the first week, you'll want to have 30 to 40 feet clear in front of you and behind you. At first, most of your casting will involve distances of 30 to 40 feet, but later you'll want the space to extend the cast.

Go where you feel comfortable. You might feel a little self-conscious at first, but you'll soon forget about that as you start to concentrate on mastering the basic cast. So much for talk. Let's begin casting. Remember, it won't all come at once.

Notice that this caster isn't holding the line under the index finger of his right hand. This is a bad habit to get into. Placing your index finger on the line gives you better control of your line.

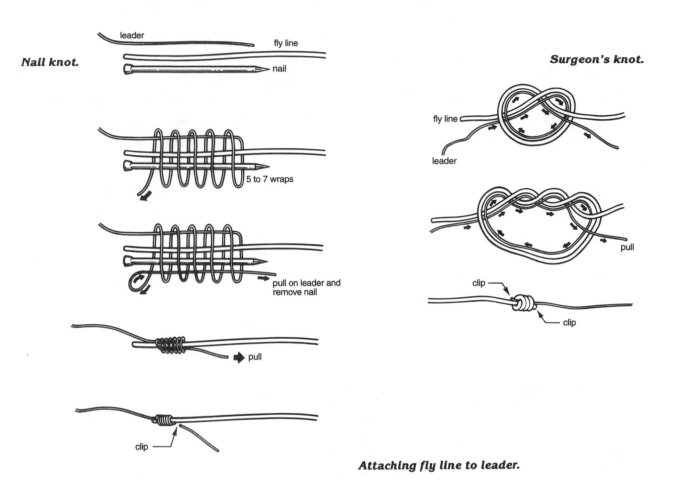

Nail knot.

leader

fly line

nail

5 to 7 wraps

pull on leader and remove nail

pull

clip

Surgeon's knot.

fly line

leader

pull

clip

clip

Attaching fly line to leader.

Beginning Casting Steps

Step A: Setting Up Your Leader, Fly Line, and Hook

1. Assemble your rod, and thread the fly line through the eyes.

2. Attach the leader to the fly line. There are a number of ways you can attach fly line to leader, but for beginning purposes, use a double surgeon's knot. Any tapered leader will do. However, for your few first practice sessions any seven- to eight-foot piece of monofilament will do. Ten-pound test off your spinning reel works well, but anything you have lying around will do the trick. For your first practices, this will be a lot cheaper than using a new leader.

3. Attach a fly or hook to the leader. If you've never attached a hook to a leader, you can refer to the discussion on knots or use any

pull to tighten

Improved cinch knot. This is the best knot to use to secure the fly to the leader. Moisten the knot with saliva before tightening it.

Position yourself directly in front of your target. Then turn 30 degrees toward your casting arm. Don't start the forward cast until your line has laid out flat behind you.

old knot that comes to mind. For practice, it doesn't matter. Now, so you won't hook your ear or give yourself a nose ornament the hard way, cut off the bottom of the hook (the point and barb) where it makes a "J" shape. Sacrificing the price of a few hooks or flies is nothing compared to the pain of hooking your ear.

4. Peel off 30 feet of line. In the center of your casting area, lay down your rod and strip off about 30 feet of line, including your leader.

Step B: Getting in Place, Holding Your Rod and Line

5. Grip the cork handle snugly, midway up the handle, with the reel facing down and your thumb pointing up the rod. You want to hold the rod snugly, but not *too* tightly. Play around and assume a grip that feels comfortable.

6. Face where you want to cast, then turn six inches to the right or left, depending on which arm you cast with. (Turn right if you cast with your right hand; turn left if you cast with your left hand.) You are standing at an angle, so you can easily look over your shoulder at your line. Remember, you want it to be entirely flattened out before you pull it forward.

7. Pick a target area you want your fly to hit. It's not critical for the first few practice sessions, but later on it's a good idea to have

something to cast to. After you master the rudiments, it might be helpful to slightly overcast—that is, aim three or four feet beyond the object. In a stream, you can always pull the fly back to your target if you overcast.

Step C: The Pickup

8. Drop the tip of your rod a foot or two toward the line that's lying on the grass. You'll be holding your rod at about the 9:00 position.

9. With your left hand (assuming you're right-handed; use your right hand if you're left-handed), take up the slack line. Simply pull the line away from your reel toward the left.

10. In a fluid, brisk motion, lift the rod up, also lifting the line off the lawn (or water). This should be a smooth motion, not a harsh yank. The line and leader will start to come off the grass.

11. When your rod reaches 11:00, put some power (smooth power) into your back cast.

Remember, you're standing next to a clock. Don't worry if the line lands at your feet the first dozen times or so. It means you probably jerked too much.

STOP: *If the line is still piling up, practice the pickup until you have it. There's no point in going further until you have mastered this step. Millions of now-brilliant fly fishers have stopped here. I was one of them.*

Step D: The 11:00-to-1:00-and-Back False Cast

12. Stop the rod tip at 1:00 and allow the line to flatten out behind you. Don't try to do a forward cast yet. Instead, make a half dozen pickups. Look over your shoulder, and watch the line come back. See how it hangs there and then drops. Watch it. Count how long it takes for the line to unroll and flatten out. This is why you are turned. Try a few more casts, watching the line.

Notice the line? This is a bad cast that can't be controlled. The caster didn't wait for the line to lay out behind him before beginning the forward cast. To complicate matters, he dropped his rod too far forward.

13. Watch the line over your shoulder. When it has flattened out, push the rod forward. If the line is flattened out, your return movement will feel crisp. You'll be able to feel the line.
14. Push the rod straight ahead until you reach 12:00, then accelerate until 11:00.

STOP: *Did you hear a snapping noise? If you did, you weren't letting the line flatten out on the back cast. Did you feel the line when you pushed? If you did, you pushed at the right time. If the line didn't fly through the air smoothly, it's likely that your timing was off. Go back and practice steps 12 through 14 again.*

15. Let the line flatten out in front of you. This part of the cast usually doesn't present a problem, because you can easily see the line.
16. Pull the rod (thus the line) straight back. Pull briskly until 12:00. Then accelerate until the rod tip is at 1:00.

RUTTER'S CASTING TIPS

- *Don't bring the rod too far back.*
- *Let your line flatten out before you start the forward cast.*
- *Don't overpower the forward cast.*
- *Put enough power into your back cast.*

---

17. Push the rod straight forward. You have just executed a *false cast*—a cast in which you don't let the line drop to the water. You will use the false cast for a number of things. Most frequently, you'll use it to dry your fly or "load line." The next step is easy.

Step E: The Actual Cast

18. Now let's cast at your target. Lift the line up, go into the back cast as before, and execute the forward cast. This time, hold the rod in the 11:00 position instead of pulling back. The line will flatten out. Let it drift softly to the ground. The "drifting softly to the ground" part takes a little practice. When you're more accomplished, you will drop your fly on the target.
19. Release the line with your left hand at the end of the 11:00 thrust. If you like, you can feed a little line out, releasing the tension with your left hand. Practice the release. This will help your line drift down.

STOP: *You have now gone through the basic cast. It's time to practice it over and over again. After half an hour on the lawn, you'll be able to hit the nearest stream.*

At the least, you should practice these steps until the process has become a smooth motion.

Here's another helpful tip: Ask a friend or significant other to watch you cast, reading you each step just before you administer it. A second set of eyes from an impartial observer will be a great help—it's hard for you to see what's happening to the line behind your back.

When to Move On

When is it time to move on? When you cast mostly right. What does "mostly right" mean? Hell, I don't know. Every person is different. But setting that disclaimer aside, I can offer a few rules to guide you in moving from one casting step to the next.

The overhead cast is fundamental in fly fishing, but you can move on whenever you like. No one is there to check up on you. I personally tend to move through things rapidly. It's part of my compulsive nature. However, as Robert Frost says in a poem, "It's often a step backward taken."

When you feel you have the basics of casting down pat—when it's a fluid motion (at least most of the time)—it's time to move on. If a heap of line is dropping at your feet, if your fly is snapping off, or if the line isn't laying straight in front or in back of you, don't go on. Practice more. Can you cast all day? If casting feels like work, you need to practice.

You'll be polishing the basic cast for a long time before you get it perfect, but it sure doesn't have to be perfect before you move ahead. You may pick up basic casting in 20 minutes or 20 hours. Everyone is different.

Loading Up Line for Long Casts

Just as discretion is the better part of valor, accuracy is the better part of casting. Casting 100 feet doesn't matter if you can't get your fly where you want it to go. Accuracy is paramount. Now that you're feeling comfortable and fluid and casting close to your target, it's time to work on adding line. Fly casters call it *loading*.

While working your false cast, you're going to add or "feed" line into your cast, allowing you to get more distance. You'll be tempted to really load up, which means you'll be trying to handle a lot of line. However, you're better off if you defy human nature and work with just five or ten feet of line at a time, continuing to cast as fluidly and accurately as possible. Being accurate is more important than dumping out lots of uncontrollable line. Your objective is to strip off extra line and feed it to your false cast.

This caster is preparing to feed line on his next cast.

Feeding Line to Your Cast. Try a couple of false casts first, to get into the swing of things. Then proceed with the following steps (directions are for right-handed casters; substitute the other hand in these steps if you're left-handed):

1. Strip off a few feet of line.
2. When your rod is lifting for the pickup (in the 11:00 position) hold the line near the reel with your left hand.
3. Let your left hand, which is holding the line, drop toward the reel slightly as you start lifting/pulling the rod back.
4. As you lift your right arm in the back cast, let your left hand come farther in toward your reel. With your left hand, make sure the line is fairly taut.
5. As you move toward 11:00 again, the "J" loop will move away from you. Now is the time to "feed" out line. Feeding is done by simply letting the line glide through your fingers. The line is being pulled forward through the eyes by the weight of the loop and the flex of the rod.
6. When the line has been threaded out and is lying flat, tighten the tension on the line with your left hand. Go again into your back cast.

This process is repeated until you have the line loaded.

Tips on Feeding Line. I may sound like a broken record, but go a few feet at a time. If you can't get the line to lay flat on your front and back casts, you are trying to work with too much line out. If the line is snapping on the back cast, it means you're pulling it forward before it has flattened out. Again, you're working with too much line. Don't spend a lot of time feeding line until you have your pickup and the basic cast under control. At this stage, if you can cast 30 or 35 feet, you're doing very well.

The Roll Cast

Sometimes you'll fish a stretch of water lined with bushes, willows, or trees. Making an *official* cast is out of the question—you'll only snag shrubbery on your back cast. You'll want to use a *roll cast*, a cast that takes place mostly in front of you. If you've bait fished or spin cast, you've probably done a modified version of the roll cast several thousand times. You just didn't know what it was called.

Why Use a Roll Cast?

Obstructions. Casting in the traditional manner (back casting) isn't always practical, because you'll probably lodge your fly in something organic—and it won't be a fish's mouth. An obstruction in the path of the back cast is the most common reason for roll casting. On smaller waters, or when you're working a tight bank, sometimes you can only cast your fly up or down the stream. You aren't able to cast from side to side without hanging yourself up.

Wet Fly Fishing. When you're fishing a weighted nymph or you've put shot on the leader, it isn't comforting to have heavy flies zipping past your ear at 200 miles per hour. It's often easier to *plop* your fly down, via a roll cast, since extreme accuracy and finesse aren't essential.

Pride. You still haven't got the back cast down the way you'd like. You feel outclassed using it in front of snobs until you've had more lawn practice. So you roll cast. I know some fly fishers who've never graduated out of roll casting. They catch plenty of fish. It's limiting, but you can catch a lot of trout with a roll cast.

Ease. Sometimes when you're thoroughly working a stretch of water, making a series of roll casts is easier than back casting.

The roll is a handy, useful cast to have in your fly fishing bag of tricks. It's easy to learn. It takes about three minutes or five tries. It's called a roll cast because that's what your line does—it rolls or makes a loop. If you think in terms of a circle, it's quite easy. Consider the following steps:

How to Do the Roll Cast

1. Your line must be in the water. You need the weight of the water on your line and fly—the tension holds both in place. Lift your rod fluidly to the 12:00 position. Some of the line will hang toward you (above the surface of the water).
2. Ease the rod back to the 1:00 position. The limp line should be hanging near your right elbow. The line will form a loop extending from the rod tip to the spot where the line enters the water.

HE SHOULD HAVE USED A ROLL CAST.

3. With a push, lifting just a little, accelerate forward to the 9:00 position. The motion will cause your fly line to make a loop, shooting the line and fly in the direction of the rod tip.

These are the major steps, but the roll cast is actually one fluid movement. You need a smooth, uniform motion to effectively cast the fly. As always, practice is the key to improvement.

Once you've gained confidence in your basic cast and your roll cast, move ahead to the next chapter, where we'll tackle new casting techniques.

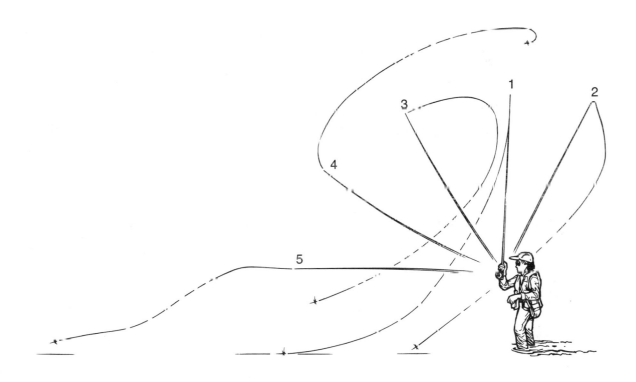

The roll cast. The numbers indicate the steps of the cast.

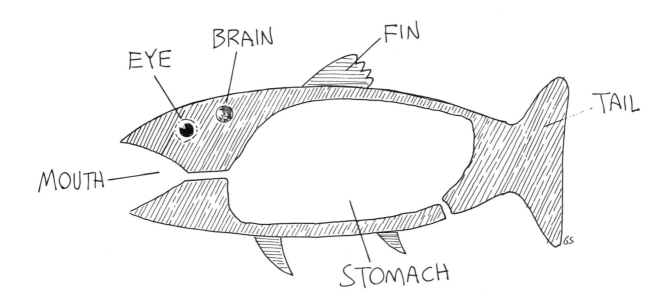

PEA BRAIN FISH — BASIC FISH ANATOMY

FIVE

Mending and Other Casts

Casting with Style

BESIDES CATCHING FISH, very few things delight a fly fisher more than showing off a wonderful casting style. In this chapter, I'll discuss how to polish your casting techniques and introduce you to other casts you'll want to add to your bag of tricks.

If you've learned the casts we talked about in Chapter 4, you can cast well. However, let's talk about another important part of casting and fly fishing; it's called *mending*.

Being a damn-fine caster who can drop a fly in a teacup at 80 feet won't help you catch fish unless you understand how your fly line, leader, and fly are floating on the water.

Mending Your Lines

Fish aren't smart. But they *are* creatures of habit. Despite their pea-sized brains, they can frustrate the hell out of the most "degreed" caster.

Remember this above all else: *Your fly, wet or dry, must always look natural when it floats on the water!* It can't drift faster or slower than the current, nor can it move at a different speed from other floating material (twigs, bubbles, foam, and the like). In fly fishing, the problem of drift is called *drag*. It's caused when the current pulls the line or leader, which in turn skates or pulls the fly unnaturally. Mending means adjusting your fly line so that the fly floats naturally, without drag. You can mend your line by throwing a mending cast or by gently pulling your line across the water.

Because a fish is a creature of habit, it knows what looks like "normal" food and what doesn't. True, a fish will chase live bugs and minnows scooting about, but most of the time the current itself brings a fish's dinner. That means aquatics or terrestrials, alive or dead, either by accident or on purpose, are swept into the current and constantly drift past our pea-brained fish's nose. The fish knows what looks like a natural drift and what doesn't. To save energy, our fish will find a comfortable spot in the stream and wait—eating whatever the current brings or whatever happens to look yummy.

Your *presentation*, first and foremost, *must drift like a real piece of fish food.* Your fly must drift in a natural manner. The correct drift is a lot more important than hav-

To mend your line, take up the slack, lift the rod, and position the belly of the line.

ing the right color, the right size, or the exact imitation. Your fly must float on the current like a piece of tasty fish lunch. Even if everything else is perfect, you won't fool most of the fish most of the time if you aren't getting the right presentation, or the right drift. As you can see, casting your fly flawlessly isn't enough.

How do you get the right drift? Mend your line with a cast, so it compensates for shifting currents when it lands on the water. Or, since your line tends to float faster than your fly, mend after the cast by shifting sections of fly line up or down the stream to compensate for the current.

Life would be easier but a lot less challenging if all the water in a stream flowed evenly. It doesn't. There are currents, eddies, back currents, and faster and slower currents—all within the drift of your fly.

Your leader might rest in a slow part of the flow, while your fly line sits in a fast current. The current will pull your line, whipping or dragging your fly unnaturally. Or perhaps your fly is in a fast current and the line is in slow water. The fly line will cause the fly to slow down unnaturally. Rarely will a fish in its right fish mind consider a fly that's drifting too fast or too slow. Fish aren't that smart, but after living on drifting food for their entire lives, they know when something doesn't drift naturally.

While you're fishing, constantly check your fly. Maybe I should reword the sentence. Check the fly's drift in the water as follows:

Dry Fly Drift. If it's a radical difference between the drift of the fly and the speed of the current, you'll notice the fly skating across the water unnaturally. To get a more subtle reading, look at a bubble drifting near your fly. Your fly should float at the same speed. If your fly moves at a different speed than the foam, bubbles, or drifting objects, you've got a problem. It's not drifting naturally.

Wet Fly Drift. It's a little hard to tell, because your fly is underwater. Often you'll be fishing with a small amount of shot. You have to adjust the amount so you'll have to experiment in each section of the water. You'll want the fly to float at the level you desire, keeping in mind that the drift may be different near the bottom than it is on the surface. Once you have the right amount of weight on, watch the line or the strike indicator. Does it float naturally?

You will need to mend often when you're casting *across* different drifts. Heavy fly line on the water will be predisposed to *belly* downstream. That is, the current will carry the heavier fly line more quickly than the lighter leader, creating drag and a "C" shaped curve in the fly line. This drag will skate your fly across the current. Sometimes when you're wet fly fishing, this is a good thing—but make sure you're doing it on purpose. For dry fly casting (except with a caddis fly), it's almost always the kiss of death.

The stronger current has pulled, or bellied,
the line between the reel and the first eye on the rod.

You can prevent drag by working with shorter, more manageable drifts and controlling the "belly" of the line. As I've suggested, you can mend several ways, depending on your skill and the current. You can mend your line while it's on the water, called *surface water mending,* or while it's in the air, by using a mending cast.

Lets look at ways to mend line on the surface, or surface water mending:

Short Mends with the Drift. With short, whipping motions of your rod, flip portions of fly line up or down the current as it's drifting and you're taking in line. Mend periodically as needed.

C-Mend (Flip the Belly Upstream). Cast four to five feet above your target area and a little farther across. As soon as the line is on the water lift and flip it upstream to prevent a belly. Actually, you're *creating* a belly in the opposite direction. With the body of the line, create a "C" shape between you and the fly.

Surface "S" Mend. After you cast, lift and throw to create a series of "S" curves in the line. This produces enough slack so that your fly will drift naturally.

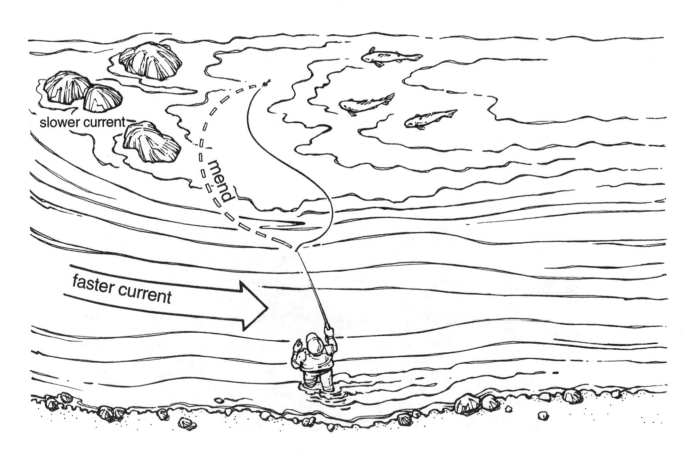

Mend upstream, so that the fly—which is in slower water—will drift naturally.

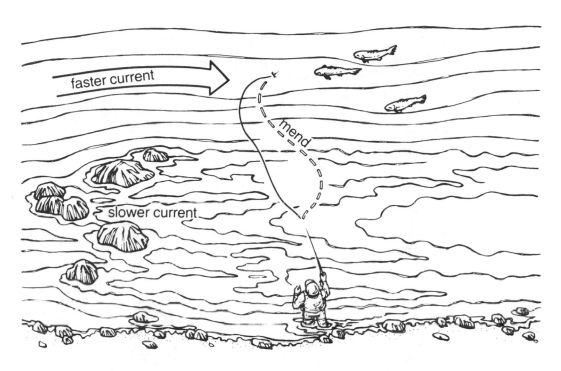

faster current

slower current

mend

Mend downstream, so that the fly—which is in faster water—will drift naturally.

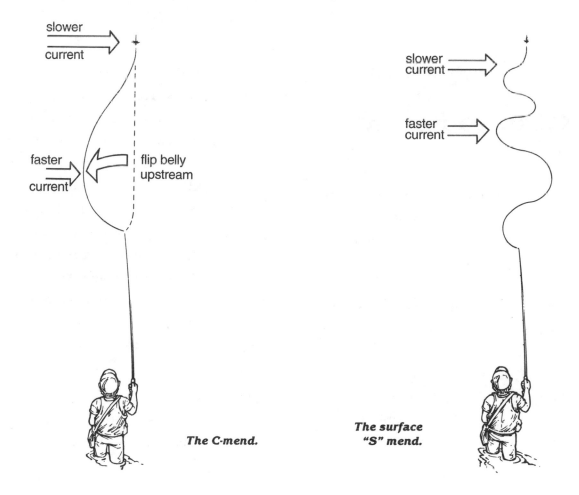

slower current

faster current

flip belly upstream

The C-mend.

slower current

faster current

The surface "S" mend.

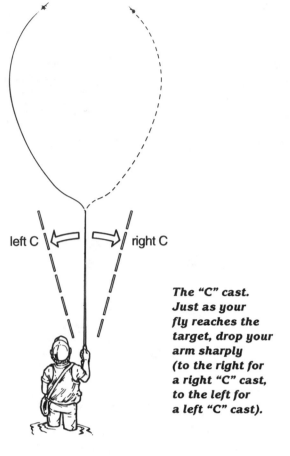

The snake cast. Before the line hits the water, shake it back and forth.

The "C" cast. Just as your fly reaches the target, drop your arm sharply (to the right for a right "C" cast, to the left for a left "C" cast).

Mending Casts You'll Be Glad to Know

Why work any harder than you have to? Why mend on the water if you can accomplish the same thing in the air? Realistically, you'll often be doing some of both. But the advantage is yours if you can mend during the cast.

How can you mend your line in the air? With a *mending* or a *slack cast*. As you've undoubtedly assumed, mending casts have the mend built in. When your line hits the water, there is already slack, so your fly drifts without drag. There will also be less water disturbance, and you can watch your fly more carefully. Let's look at several mending casts.

Snake Cast. The most common is called a *snake cast*. It takes a little practice, but it's an effective way to throw a mend into your line. Practice on the lawn a few times to get the rudiments down pat. Remember that the line does what the rod tells it to do.

Before the line hits the water, instead of bringing your arm down straight, throw a series of wiggles or shivers into the line by moving the rod from side to side. You can control how large you want your curves by how much you move your arm from left to right. The greater the curves, the longer the drag-free drift.

"C" Cast. Another mending cast is called the "C" or *curve cast*. You can cast slack to your left or right, depending on what is needed. Most often, you'll want the curve in the line to be upstream from you and the fly. The line curves, forming a "C" shape that allows a natural drift.

False cast a time or two to get out the line you need. As your arm is pulling forward, reaching the 11:00 position, move it to the right and bring it slightly back. The more you move your arm to the right, the larger the curve. The longer you pause before dropping the rod, the closer to you the "C" will be.

It takes about 20 minutes of practice, but it's not hard to learn. Practice casting by moving your arm six inches to two feet to the right or left, so you can predict how far away and how large the curve is. After 20 casts, you'll be feeling confident.

Steeple Cast. What would you call a high cast that goes almost straight up, especially if you played hooky from Sunday school so you could fish? You'd call it a steeple cast, of course.

Every now and then, there's an obstruction behind you, and it's impossible to use any sort of back cast. A roll cast won't give you enough distance. If you let your line stray, even a little, you'll have a monstrous tangle.

The stretch of water looks very promising. You decide to cast back and up, so the fly shoots overhead like a steeple, then arches

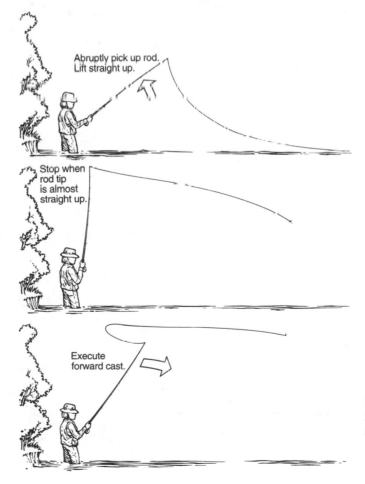

The steeple cast allows the caster to fish next to bushes or trees.

Most fly casters mend too late. Keep an eye on your fly, and position your line before drag occurs.

down. Because you're casting high, you're avoiding the stuff behind you, but you're still able to fish the water in front of you. You will use the steeple cast as you fish edges of ponds and lakes and the banks of rivers and streams. Follow these steps when steeple casting:

1. Lay the line on the water. Then lift the rod with an abrupt wrist pickup, followed by an accelerated and full arm movement. The middle and tip portions of your rod assume a lot of the work, powering the line up.
2. When the line has reached its apex (more or less directly above your head), an accurately executed front cast will rifle your line and fly where you desire.

Modifications of the Back Cast

As we discussed in Chapter 4, the back cast will serve you well most of the time. But not always. We've talked about obstructions and introduced the steeple cast. However, there is another obstacle a fly caster has to face—and face often. That obstacle is the wind.

At first, you might think the never-ending wind is the biggest pain in a fly caster's life, taking most of the fun out of throwing a fly. Later, as you perfect your back cast, you'll realize that you can cast in progressively stronger winds. Maybe you can't throw quite as much line, but you've learned to make sure your back line is straight, to hesitate longer, to accelerate with a little more power, to make your loops tighter, and to position yourself advantageously.

But sometimes all that just ain't enough! The wind gets a little too strong, and you can't quite get your fly where you want it. What do you do?

Cast low. The wind is stronger at chest level than at knee level. Likewise, the wind is stronger at rod tip (13 to 15 feet) than at chest level. When you cast overhead, you encounter a fair amount of wind resistance.

It's time to do what is called a *side cast* or *wind cast*. A side cast is like an overhead cast, but it's executed at your side. This cast keeps your line low and out of strong wind currents. If you have the overhead cast under control, it will take you only a few minutes to master the side cast. Simply take your rod from the vertical plane (the overhead cast) and put it in the horizontal plane. Instead of casting over your head, cast at your side.

You'll still want to cast from 11:00 to 1:00. In your mind's eye, because you're casting on the horizontal plane, imagine that the clock has tilted back. It, too, is now on the horizontal plane.

Once you have the right side cast down, try casting on your left. Reach over to your left side with your right arm, and master the side cast on your left side. The ability to cast on both sides is handy.

Final Casting Observations

None of the casts we've looked at are difficult, especially if you have the back cast under control. All it takes is practice. When you're practicing on your lawn, work through the various casts. Or when you're fishing and the fish aren't cooperating, throw a few practice lines. Whip a few snake casts and a few side casts. Then throw a few steeple casts. Practice, practice, practice. It can be fun, fun, fun.

The bottom line when selecting a fly is hooking a fish.

SIX

The Fly Itself

Psychology of Dry and Wet

MONUMENT TO THE TIED FLY

FLIES ARE FISHED EITHER *DRY* OR *WET*. Dry flies are fished on the film, the top layer of the water. Wet flies are fished between the film and the bottom.

Psychology of Fly Casting Dry and Wet

Dry Fly Casters. When a snobbish dry fly caster looks at the water, all she sees is the film, the hatch, and the fish rising.

A dry fly purist will fish only the film, and she will feel morally superior to anyone who doesn't share her casting orientation. She knows a dry fly presentation should be perfect. Such a caster revels in her quest for the perfect cast, and thus the perfect trout. If she can't catch fish on the film, she'll haughtily declare that the fish aren't yet worth catching, and she'll gladly wait patiently until they rise (even if it takes until next spring).

A dry fly caster almost always has a superior cast. She frequently takes fly fishing to the extreme—wearing the best clothes, choosing the best gear, looking like the ultimate yuppie. However, don't call her bluff when it comes to throwing a perfect loop. She can drop a #22 fly on a quarter at 107 feet.

67

Such a caster will gladly fish all day to ensure that she's on the water for that enchanted 15 or 20 minutes when a hatch occurs. Matching the hatch exactly and catching one fish, even a small one, makes it all worthwhile.

Wet Fly Casters. When the wet fly snob looks at the water, all he sees is the structure on the bottom, the underwater currents, and a very large trout hiding on the lee side of a boulder.

Wet fly casting isn't as technically difficult as dry fly fishing, but there are always fish to catch. Many casters get hooked on wet casting and never leave it. They like catching lots of trout even if they have to go underwater to do it, thus violating the purist's sensibilities. The wet fly caster has gotten so sidetracked by wet fly fishing that he's forgotten about the surface film and the attractive woman who's casting a perfect loop. Instead, he concentrates on how he can get his fly to that big fish.

The wet fly caster has an okay cast, but it doesn't need to be as refined, perfected, or as pretty as his counterpart's cast. An average caster might be a fairly good wet fly fisher. Some never get past the roll cast and the lob. When you're fishing with weighted flies or you have lead on the line, a cast becomes more of a directed pitch. It doesn't matter if the fly or the line slaps the water, because the fish don't care—they're down deep. You still have drift worries, but they're not as problematic.

A wet fly caster casts in order to get the job done. A dry fly caster casts because she likes to hear the delicate swish of line over her head and enjoys casting for its own sake.

This steelhead was taken on a dry fly—a Royal Coachman.

This steelhead was taken on a wet fly—a Woolly Bugger.

A Little Bit of Both. There are those snobs, like me, who want the best of both worlds. Why not have your casting cake and eat it, too? If you're like most casters, you'll probably find yourself throwing both wet and dry—especially if you like to catch fish. It's nice to be a romantic fly thrower like the dry caster, but it's even nicer to be a fly angler who catches fish.

Here's my advice: When the fish are feeding on the surface, fish dry flies. When they aren't, fish wet flies. Go where the fish are, and present flies they'll take.

There's no doubt that most casters love to see a fish rise to a dry fly. It's the ultimate rush. However, fish don't always feed on the surface. In fact, most of the time they feed on the bottom. If you wait until they bust the film, you might wait a long time. This is why a dry fly

purist has such a good cast. When there aren't fish on the film, which is often, casting practice is in order. These folks cast to drifting foam and bits of wood, pretending the flotsam is a rising fish.

Wet fly folks get a lot more action, because they go directly to the fish. Also, wet fly casters generally don't have to be as selective about patterns or presentation. A fish's feeding habits under the film are more random and opportunistic. Fish aren't as nervous. When they're near the surface, danger is always present, but they're safer underwater. When you're using a wet fly, your fly size should be somewhat close to the ideal, but you don't have to be exact. Color usually isn't that critical, either. Instead you need to get near the bottom and present a natural drift. The correct drift is essential for

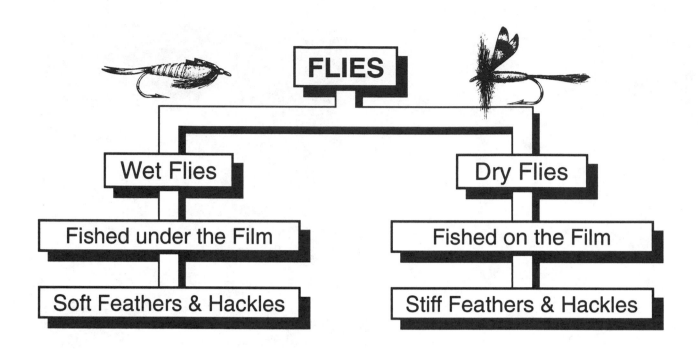

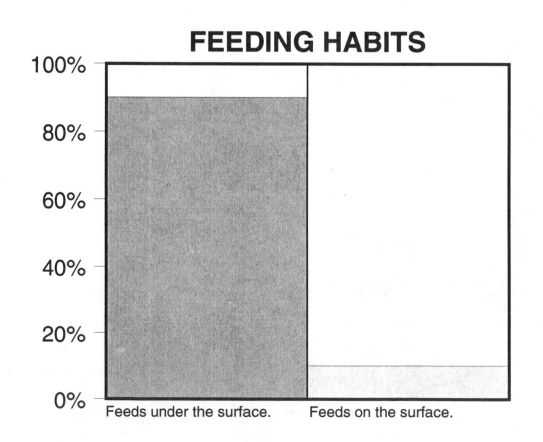

both types of casting. On the film or on the bottom, your fly must look like something good to eat and be presented realistically—which means it must drift naturally in the current.

Fish a little of both. There's a bit of the snob dry caster in all of us, but there's a wet caster in there, too.

Anatomy of Dry and Wet Flies

A dry fly is fished on the film. A wet fly is fished *under* the film. This seems obvious, but some flies cross over effectively and are fished both wet and dry. For example, an Adams is primarily a dry fly, but it can be successfully fished wet. A Coachman or a Wulff is a dry attractor fly (a nonspecific fly), but it can be deadly when fished wet. An ant or a hopper is usually fished dry, but it can be fished wet as well. An Elk Hair Caddis is a dry fly, but it can be fished like a streamer. There are dozens of other examples.

Physical elements help determine whether a fly is, in theory, fished wet or dry. The most noticeable is the *hackle*, the feather collar near the eye of the hook. A dry fly hackle holds it up in the water. Its feathers often come from the neck or saddle of a mature rooster that's harvested in the spring, when plumage is best. The feathers are stiff, shiny, and fully fibered, and they narrow to a point. The colors might be white, gray (grizzly), red, black, or mixed. A wet fly hackle is not as pronounced, and the feathers are generally soft. This hackle may be made from a rooster, but hen feathers are preferred because they're softer.

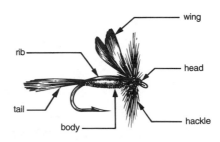

Anatomy of a dry fly.

Dry Flies. A dry fly is a rather bushy fly, because of its pronounced hackle. If you drop it, it will usually land sitting erect. A dry fly needs to float or ride on the film in a delicate manner. It simulates an insect that, for one reason or another, has landed on the water. It's suspended in the water by a cock hackle.

The *dry fly hackle*, a bottle-brush-looking affair, is wound in a circle just behind the eye of the hook. It suspends the fly on the water and mimics a bug's legs and wings.

The *skater hackle* is constructed with long hackle to keep the hook out of the water.

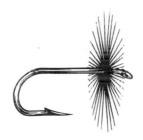

A dry fly's hackle helps the fly float properly on the water and gives the fly a "leggy" look.

Skater hackle, a more extended hackle, allows the hook to ride high on the film. It also allows the pattern to move naturally in the current when moved by the rod.

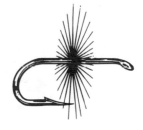

Palmered hackle supports the dry fly and gives added body to the wet fly.

The *palmered hackle* is a famous, traditional design. The hackle is secured down the shank of the hook to give the fly additional support.

On its own, a dry fly will float for a short time until the feathers soak up moisture. To keep it floating longer, a dry caster will apply a dressing on the fly so it won't absorb water. This dressing is called *floatant*. If you treat your fly before it's initially wet, it will stay dry longer.

In a pinch, when you're out of floatant, a series of dry casts will dry your fly.

You will generally use a longer leader when you fish a dry fly. Depending on the conditions, the leader may be 9 to 12 feet long. You'll want more distance between the fly line and the fly, so you don't spook the fish.

Wet Flies. A wet fly is generally more slender and streamlined. If you drop it on a table, it will land with a *clunk* on its side. These flies must slice through the water and look lifelike. Or they need to dead drift (float naturally, without drag, in the current) the way a natural water bug would if it had been drowned or swept away. A wet fly is sometimes tied with a small amount of hen hackle to make it look more

The Coachman pattern is a popular dry fly. It's bushy, and it's designed to float on the film.

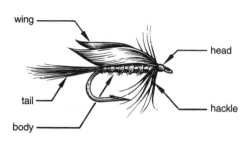

wing

head

tail

hackle

body

Anatomy of a wet fly.

Streamers are typically brightly colored and "flowing" in the water—perhaps imitating bait fish or leeches.

alive in the water. There are several types of wet flies. The categories are generic, and they overlap somewhat.

The *wet fly* can simulate a variety of food—a drowned bug (ant, hopper), an emerging nymph, a female depositing eggs, or a small fish.

Streamers imitate a generic bait fish or fry. They are attractor patterns that don't really look like anything. These flies can be easily identified because they're tied on a long-shanked hook. A Muddler Minnow, a Woolly Bugger, a Leech, and a Mickey Finn are examples.

The Leech is one of my favorite wet fly patterns.

*The nymph is an imitation
of underwater aquatic life.*

A *nymph* is an impression of an aquatic bug. Aquatics are a major portion of a fish's diet. There are two basic stages, the larva and the emerger, in which the insect heads for the surface. The Pheasant Tail, the Zug Bug, the Light Cahill, and the Hare's Ear are popular patterns.

Fishing a Wet Fly. You can see a fish take a dry fly, so you'll know roughly when to set the hook. When you fish a wet fly, you're more or less fishing blind. After you've fished for a while, you'll get a feel for when you should set the hook. In the meantime, set the hook whenever you feel a hesitation, a stop, a jolt, a bump, or an unnatural change in line direction. You'll set the hook falsely a number of times, but you'll also catch more fish. The fish's "bite" is soft and easy to miss. When in doubt, set your hook by lifting the rod.

When you start fishing wet, and maybe until you're an expert, a *strike indicator* is a useful tool. The strike indicator is a small float attached to your leader. The slightest pressure will pull it under like a bobber, so you'll know when to set the hook. It lets you know when a fish picks up your fly and when to put tension on the line. You'll often want your fly to drift

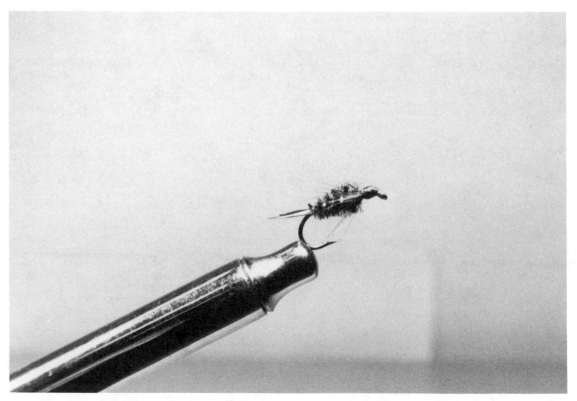

The Prince Nymph, a popular wet fly. It's streamlined and looks lifelike underwater.

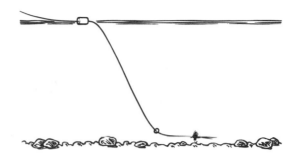

The strike indicator is the wet fly caster's bobber. Watch the indicator. If it shifts direction contrary to the current or if it goes under, lift the rod to set the hook.

right across the bottom. To make it do this, put lead shot a few inches above the fly or use a weighted pattern. You'll set the strike indicator from three to six feet up the leader, depending on the depth of the water and the current. A good rule of thumb, allowing for current differences, is twice the depth of the water. You don't want the indicator so low that it's constantly pulled under, or so high that the line is too slack. You'll have to adjust the distance as you fish different sections of current. The strike indicator should float across the top of the water.

As you work the drift, keep an eye on the strike indicator. If it moves in any way, or if it goes under, set the hook. You may get a lot of false strikes because of the currents or rocks, but you'll catch fish, too. A wet fly pickup, or bite, is very subtle.

You will generally use a short leader on a wet fly. I start at 7 feet. Because the fly is underwater, you don't have to worry quite so much about spooking the fish with your line. A short leader gives you more control.

The Woolly Bugger is one of the most deadly flies ever tied.

COUNTER DECEPTION

SEVEN

Platonic Entomology
A Crash Course in Bugs

*Selecting the right fly could make the difference
between catching fish and not catching them.*

KNOWLEDGE OF BUGS SEPARATES THE CASUAL FLY FISHER FROM THE REALLY *SERIOUS* FLY FISHER. In this chapter and the next, we'll get down to serious fly fishing.

The Nature of Plato and Copying

Fly casting is copying. And because it is, it's Platonic in nature. Plato taught us there is an ideal prototype for everything that ex-

ists. This ideal concept first existed in the mind of God. From this concept, God created the first physical realization of the ideal prototype. Everything on earth is a copy (or a copy of that copy) of that ideal prototype, which exists with God on his ideal plane. Which brings us back to fly fishing. When we duplicate an insect, we are making copies of the ideal. The better job we do, the closer we come to the original prototype—

and the more fish we're likely to catch. You might say that a good copy is our business, our lifeblood, and our passion. We try to duplicate skillfully, so we can fool that big brown with our facsimile—the fly. But, you can't make flies, select flies, fish, or appreciate this whole notion of "copying" if you don't understand what you're mimicking.

Musical Flies. In the good old days, when I ripped off my father's fly box, I didn't have a clue. I took a quick glance, saw what looked good, plucked it up, and lashed it on my tippet. I caught fish, but I also endured some fishless days. It was a random crap shoot. "I like red," I'd say to myself. "This fly's got a red tail. I'll use it."

I was playing musical flies. Like musical chairs, the musical flies approach works in a chaotic sort of way. You might get the exact right bug and get lucky. Or the fish might be very aggressive, slamming everything that comes its way. You might get the correct fly size or chance into the right pattern. But getting lucky isn't enough. At least not for a serious fly fisher.

The random approach yields an occasional fish—enough, in fact, to keep a caster going. I fished this way for five or six years. But here's the bottom line, so to speak: If you don't understand what's going on in the water, you leave too much to chance. Presenting flies that the fish are going for dramatically increases your chances of being successful on a regular basis. When you know your flies, you're fishing with a strategy.

Don't play musical flies any more than you have to. In order to help you fish the right insect, let's take a look at bugs and their cycles. First, we'll consider the bugs most important to trout—the mayfly and the caddis fly. Next we'll look at the stone fly, the midge, crustaceans, and terrestrials.

Entomology

Entomology is the study of bugs, but for us, it's the study of bugs with a purpose. The purpose, besides matching the hatch, is to know what is going on so we can fish with a strategy. We'd like to give the fish what the fish wants.

Carrying a variety of patterns will help you match the hatch.

Turning over rocks is an excellent way to see which insects are active.

For our purposes, bugs can be divided into two categories:

1. *Water Bugs.* Aquatics, or insects that spend a portion of their lives in the water and some part on the land (mayflies, caddis flies, stone flies, midges, crustaceans).

2. *Land Bugs.* Terrestrials, or insects that spend a portion of their lives on land and have somehow fallen into the drink accidentally (hoppers, ants, beetles, bees, butterflies).

Sometimes identification is easy—the bug lands on your hat.

Aquatics: The Water Bugs

We run into problems with the aquatics. At first, they all look alike. Unless you've fly fished or your mother or father was a science teacher at the local high school, you probably lumped aquatics into "those damn bugs" you slapped at when you were tying spinners or globbing on Power Bait. Overall, most of us are pretty insect-ignorant, which is why "matching the hatch" is difficult. Everything looks alike.

Once you understand each type of fly, including its life cycle and patterns, you'll have an easier time matching it. In this chapter, we'll look at the water bugs that play an important role in successful fly casting. We'll cover the various stages of each insect, then I will suggest flies that imitate each stage.

The Mayfly. The Latin name for the taxonomic order that includes the mayfly is Ephemeroptera, which means something along the lines of "living but a day." I should qualify it by noting that most *adult* forms live only a day.

Here are some things to remember: The mayfly is an important trout meal. According to some esteemed trout historians, it's probably the first insect that early fly casters tried to duplicate. Even today, the mayfly is undoubtedly the most often duplicated pattern. Depending on who you believe, there are 300 to 500 subspecies of mayfly in different sizes and colors. But despite all the variations, a mayfly's life is fairly simple. It's divided into four stages: egg, nymph, dun (subimago), and spinner (imago).

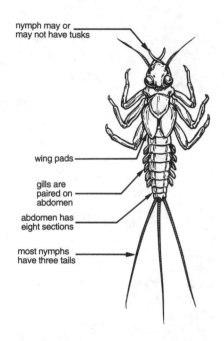

nymph may or may not have tusks

wing pads

gills are paired on abdomen

abdomen has eight sections

most nymphs have three tails

A mayfly nymph. The larval stage is called a nymph. This insect will molt 15 to 20 times. There are many variations of the nymph form.

Like any good bug, the mayfly starts its life as an egg. The female deposits her eggs on the water. The eggs then settle to the bottom or are swept downstream, where they settle into the rocks or structure.

The few eggs that survive hatch into underwater trout food called nymphs. Mayfly nymphs usually have three tails and abdominal gills. A nymph's size will vary from 4 mm to 35 mm, depending upon the water and the constraints of the ecosystem. While the color phases will vary, this nymph is usually some shade of brown. During the nymph stage, the little critters go through several growth phases called molts. Each stage allows the nymph to grow larger. This goes on for about a year. Nymphs fall into several general categories that a clever fly caster needs to be aware of:

1) *Swimmers*. These nymphs swim about freely in the water looking for nymph food and avoiding hungry fish. They are somewhat bullet-shaped, and they move in quick, darting motions.
2) *Burrowers*. These nymphs live in slow water. They like fine gravel and silty areas. They're easy to recognize, because they have tusklike extensions coming from their heads.
3) *Clingers*. These hearty nymphs live under rocks in fast, aerated water. They have a pronounced, flat shape.
4) *Crawlers*. These nymphs are oval-shaped and live on the bottom.

All good things come to an end. Mating urges call, and the nymph emerges from its watery world. Fly fishers call this "coming out." When it hears the call of the wild, the nymph emerger swims up to the surface. Its skeletal shell splits at the thorax, and a winged bug called a mayfly is born. Identifying the adult form is easy, because mayflies have a long abdomen and a tail. This critter is called a *subimago* by technical folks, but most fly casters lovingly call it the *dun*. When the wings are back, they look like sails.

A dun is a dull-looking insect with opaque wings and a tail about the length of its body. Splitting from the shell is hard work, so the dun will rest on the surface film to catch its breath and, most importantly, to dry its wings. At this time it's very helpless and is subject to preying trout. This often triggers a feeding frenzy. The birds have a feast, too. Many duns are eaten. Those that remain head for the bottoms of leaves and nearby foliage. Here they

rest, but many fall prey to aerial predators. Some tumble back into the water. After three to six hours, the dun sheds its "dun" shell. It's now fully grown, and it's called a *spinner*.

Technically called *imagoes*, spinners are duns that have cast off their dull skins for shiny new ones. Their opaque wings have become transparent. Spinners are often dark, with charcoal wings and dark olive or brown bodies. The females often have noticeable eggs on their abdomen. The tails on spinners are large. So are the eyes.

A spinner is a sexually mature mayfly. Within a day, the spinner will leave the trees or foliage, return to the water to mate, and drop over dead. It engages in a frenzied mating dance that consists of a seemingly indiscriminate series of frenetic movements, reminiscent of a disco. The fertilized female dips her abdomen in the water and expels her eggs and the cycle starts anew. Exhausted after so much living, the male and female fall into the stream and die. At this point they are often called *spent-wing spinners*. While floating on the film, they again become prey to hungry fish—often exciting another feeding frenzy.

The mayfly dun. The mayfly's upright wings look like sails. Duns have opaque wings; spinners have translucent wings.

*This dainty insect
is a mayfly.*

Flies to Match the Mayfly Hatch.
Matching the Nymph:

Hare's Ear: tan, olive (yellow in the East) body; this is an impressionistic fly, so I like to fish it large, from #12-16 hook size.

Pheasant Tail: standard brown (also yellows, red, blue); this is an imitative fly that I like to fish a little smaller, from #16-20.

March Brown, Light Cahill (nymph), Hendrickson AP Series Flies: from #12-20.

When you're nymph fishing, bounce the fly, touch the bottom regularly, or dead drift between the bottom and the surface, using the right lead or steel shot for the current (positioned 12 to 14 inches from the fly). I take a simplified approach to nymph fishing. I've never worried about trying to exactly match the various nymph types, because it gives me a headache. Trout are rarely that selective. You just need to get in the general ball park.

Matching the Emerging Mayfly:

> *Pheasant Tail:* from #14-20.
>
> *Blue-Wing Olive:* clip its wings and hackle off the bottom; from #14-20.
>
> *CDC Emerger:* from #14-20.

When you're matching the emerger, fish at a dead drift right beneath the film with a greased line (apply floatant to the leader). The fly gets soaked, but the leader helps hold it just under the surface. Clipping the wings and the hackle will help the fly ride lower in the water.

Matching the Dun:

> *Blue-Wing Olive:* from #14-20.
>
> *Light Cahill (dry):* from #12-18.
>
> *Pale Morning Dun:* from #14-20.
>
> *Quill Gordon:* from #10-16.
>
> *Adams:* from #12-22.

I use the Blue-Wing Olive two or three times more often than all the other dun flies put together—especially during the month-long spring and fall hatches. It works for me. The Adams, which is now mostly thought of as an attractor, is my second favorite. Fish on the film, at a dead drift, and pay special attention to drag.

Matching the Spinners:

> *Rusty Dun:* from #14-20.
>
> *Trico Pattern:* white wing and a black body, or a tan body; from #16-22.
>
> *Coffin Fly:* a white fly (mostly an Eastern pattern); from #6-10.

These flies often have a rusty body and clear bluish wings. Study the flies that live on the specific water you're fishing, and match accordingly. For all the insects and stages introduced in this chapter, there are a number of color variations. I try to get as close to the color as I can, but I think exact size is more important.

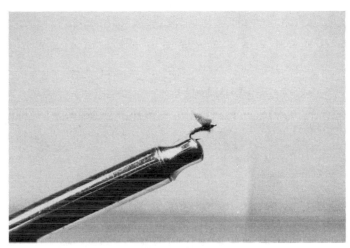

The Blue Wing Olive with sponge wings.

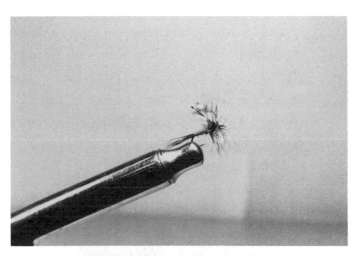

The Adams, probably one of the most popular flies in America.

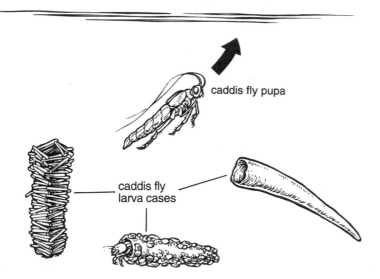

caddis fly pupa

caddis fly
larva cases

Pre-adult stages of the caddis fly.

The Caddis Fly. The caddis fly is in the order Trichoptera. Trichoptera means something like "hair on the wings." To make matters interesting, there are over 650 different species. To make matters even more interesting, there's evidence that the caddis fly population is on the increase. They apparently cope with environmental pollution effectively. Some studies suggest that mayflies may not be so hardy. They may be decreasing as a result of environmental changes.

Caddis wings are larger than their bodies. A caddis fly's flight is jerky and erratic, with no apparent smoothness or sense of purpose. Unlike the mayfly, this water critter has a "complete" life cycle, because it has two underwater stages. The adult can easily be distinguished by its tentlike wings. Let's look at the caddis's cycle: egg, larva, pupa, adult.

Zillions of caddis eggs are deposited in the water. Some beat the odds and hatch.

The next stage, the larva, is a wormlike bug. Most larvae build a case for themselves at the bottom of the drink, often in the rocks. This protective shell is composed of bits of gravel, sand, and leaf particles or small bits of wood—all held together by a cement that the insect secretes. Several types of larva don't build cases until the end of the larval stage, when they are called "free" larvae. Somewhere along the line, the larva gets the urge to construct a cocoon or retreat to its case. It's preparing for its next stage of development, pupation.

The next step in the fly's life cycle is called the pupal stage. It takes place after a year, give or take a few months. The pupa emerges from its cocoon and makes the short but very dangerous trip up from the bottom, rising through trout-infested water to the film. As you'd suspect, the pupa is vulnerable at this point. Some types ascend in trapped gas bubbles. Others crawl, swim, or dart. Many of them line trout bellies and never live to see the light of day.

Once on the film, caddis flies often flit about frenetically, never realizing how tempting they must look to fish. They are preparing to take to the air. Some hit the surface and fly away almost instantly. Either way, trout feed heavily at this time.

The adult caddis. Notice that the wings are shaped like a tent.

Unlike the adult mayfly, an adult caddis can live for several weeks to a month. Mating occurs most commonly in the late afternoon. Sometimes it occurs while they're at rest, but it often takes place in the air. Afterwards, the female deposits her eggs in the water, sometimes actually diving to the bottom. The cycle starts anew.

Flies to Match the Caddis Hatch.

Matching the Larva:

Chamois Caddis: from #12-18.

Muskrat Nymph: from #12-18.

Hare's Ear: from #12-20.

Fur Nymph: from #12-18.

Serendipity: from #12-20.

When matching the larva, the Chamois Caddis and the Serendipity are my two favorites—followed closely by the Hare's Ear. Fish in a dead drift and watch the drag.

Matching the Pupa:

La Fontain Sparkle Caddis: from #12-16.

Sedge Pupa: from #12-16.

Matching the Adult:

Elk Hair Caddis: from #12-18.

Goddard: floats really well in rough water; from #12-18.

Adams: although thought of as an attractor, this fly was first dressed to imitate a caddis adult; from #12-20.

For adult caddis fishing, all three of these flies are excellent choices. I'm partial to the Elk Hair Caddis, especially in calm water. The Goddard rides better in rough water. What can you say about the Adams? It's remarkably versatile. Fish at a dead drift, and watch the drag.

Chamois Caddis.

The Elk Hair Caddis.

An adult stone fly.

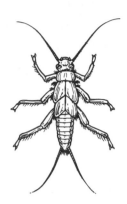

A stone fly nymph.

The Stone Fly. The stone fly, in the order Plecoptera, is the chosen bug of the fly casting *crème de la crème*. Somehow, the stone fly epitomizes the perfection of the holy art of casting. There are fishing societies that bear its name, and some big lunkers can be lured in from the depths by nothing less.

In some places, large, salmon-colored stone flies are lovingly referred to as salmon flies.

The stone fly is not a slow-water bug. It likes a swift flow and water that's very oxygenated and rocky. Let's look at the egg, nymph, and adult.

Stone fly husks on a rock. Large orange stone flies are referred to as salmon flies.

Stone fly eggs are deposited in the water by a fertilized female as she is resting.

Stone fly nymphs can live in the water for quite a long time—from one to four years. They can be distinguished from other nymphs by their antennae and the gills between their legs (not on the abdomen). They are usually large, and they have a double wing case (a double set of wings).

When the time is right, nymphs crawl out of the water. The nymph rests on a rock, a log, or a handy branch, and the winged stone fly emerges. The adult has four wings, and sometimes when the bug flies, it looks at cross-purposes. While the stone fly is mating and depositing its eggs, the trout go crazy. Since the stone fly is often good-sized, even the largest trout get into the act. The water can literally bubble with greedy fish sucking in fly after fly. It's easy to understand why this almost blind feeding frenzy would incite another frenzy—a fly fisher frenzy. When this hatch is on, casters flock to the water in droves.

Flies to Match the Stone Fly Hatch.
Matching the Nymph:
> *Box Canyon Stone:* from #4-10.
> *Gold Ribbed Hare's Ear:* from #4-16.
> *Bitch Creek:* from #4-12.

The Box Canyon Stone is the choice of most stone fly nymph fishers. The Bitch Creek is also excellent. I use the Box Canyon Stone and carry a number of Gold Ribbed Hare's Ear—which can also be used in many other situations. For success, keep your casts short, so you can feel the bottom

The Stimulator, a stone fly pattern.

and pickups. Use a six- to eight-pound leader, about eight feet long.

Matching the Adult:
> *Stimulators:* from #4-10.
> *Improved Sofa Pillow:* from #4-10.
> *Elk Hair Caddis:* from #8-12.

The Improved Sofa Pillow (strange name, isn't it?) floats very much like an adult stone fly. I like to fish pockets of likely water next to the banks at a dead drift. If this doesn't work, try what we call the Flaming Gorge Twitch—a series of small jerks, stripping in the fly line as you pull.

Midges. Midges are small bugs with two small wings. Technically, they're in the order Diptera. However, the word "midge" has become almost generic. In many casters' minds it means "small bug, trout frenzy, and slow water."

Midges are important trout food, and they can be seen in great swarms near the water. You've probably slapped hundreds of them in the first minutes of fishing trips on warm summer evenings. Midges go through a complete cycle: eggs, larva, pupa, adult. The pupa goes to the surface and floats. The winged adult later emerges. All the while, both the rising pupa and the adult are easy prey for hungry fish.

Fishing with midges is tough. Many casters work on it only after they've mastered the basics. Most often, midges are fished on clear, tricky water, like spring creeks. A caster generally needs a very light rod, at least 10 to 13 feet of leader, and a very light tippet. Also needed are perfect casts and perfect drifts. Remember, these are often limestone or spring creeks we're dealing with, which means spooky trout.

But that's the easy part. You also have to match the midge size almost perfectly.

Midging is fun, but it takes a while to get everything lined up. It's a challenging, sophisticated game.

Flies to Match the Midge Hatch.
Matching a Midge Emerger:
   Pheasant Tail: clip off the leg; from #18-24.
   Serendipity: from #18-24.
   Griffith's Gnat: clip off the hackle; from #18-22.

Don't overlook the midge emerger. Fish the fly "in" the film, just under the surface. Clipping off the legs of the Pheasant Tail and trimming the bottom of the Griffiths Gnat helps them ride low, just under the surface of the water. Size and silhouette are more important than color. Fish at a dead drift.

Matching the Adult:
   Griffith's Gnat: from #18-24.
   Adams: from #18-22.

As you know, these insects are very small. Both the Griffiths Gnat and the Adams are excellent choices (and excellent attractor flies). Carry plenty of small flies. I've listed flies up to #24, but that's very small. Anything over #20 or #22 is hard to pull off without lots of practice—it's really hard to hook the fish after it strikes. I'd stay with #20 or maybe #22, most of the time. You get fewer pickups, but you hook more fish. Use very light leader and plan on losing a lot of flies.

Crustaceans. These are hard-shelled bugs, including scuds, shrimp, crayfish, sow bugs, and cress bugs. They live on the bottom.

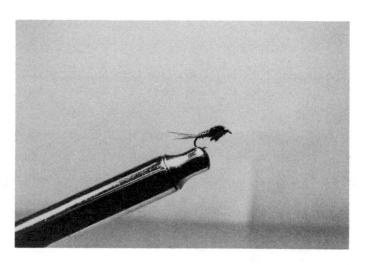

The Pheasant Tail, one of the most versatile wet flies.

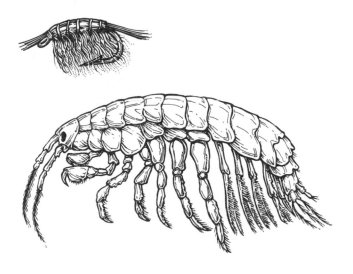

The scud, a freshwater shrimp.

Notice the freshwater shrimp in this caster's hand?
To duplicate them, you would use a fly called a scud.

To the fly caster interested in trout, the *scud* is probably the most important crustacean. A scud imitation can be used almost anytime with success. A scud is a small shrimp look-alike that lives in stream vegetation and is eaten year-round by hungry trout. If there is little surface activity and you're not sure what to tie on, a scud is always a good initial choice. You want to bump it across the bottom of the stream, putting on just enough shot so it will drift naturally.

Getting in the ballpark with size is important. Getting the right color is helpful, but not essential. Kick over a few rocks and weeds, and screen what floats down. Then match from your box, and watch what happens. When you're matching scuds, you can use grays, olives, tans, pinks, and amber, from #12-16. Gray is the most important.

Crayfish aren't as important to trout fishermen, but they *are* useful to the bass angler. We've found four-inch crays inside a 17-inch rainbow. They eat small crayfish. A brown woolly bugger is a good imitation, fished in short strips.

Terrestrials: The Land Bugs

It took me a while to wake up and smell the hot chocolate. But eventually, I discovered the terrestrial big three: ants (flying ants), grasshoppers, and beetles. What a difference it made.

If you like big fish, consider terrestrials. They are the most underused patterns in fly fishing. Unlike a politician's promise, they can be relied upon. When I'm facing a very specific hatch and I don't have the exact fly, or I think I'm matching it but I can't get a pickup, I tie on a big, juicy terrestrial. *POW.*

Terrestrials are land bugs that accidentally wind up in the drink—generally due to a gust of wind or a miscalculation in flight. Fish, being predators of opportunity, gladly take such tasty meals whenever the occasion arises . . . usually taking them with an avaricious passion.

As I suggested, even when a fish is feeding specifically on small stuff, a terrestrial can be an excellent choice. The terrestrial insect is a lot larger, but fish know a good meal when they see one, and they're liable to go for it. An assortment of terrestrials is a necessary tool in

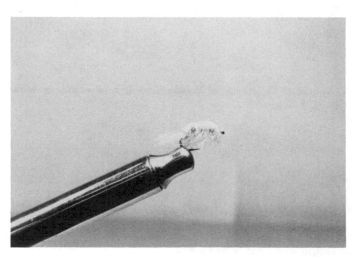

The Scud, a freshwater shrimp pattern.

your fly fishing bag of tricks. I carry a good selection in different sizes. Don't leave home without 'em.

I used to carry terrestrials in one section of my fly box. After a while, I discovered I liked fishing these land bugs (and not just when nothing else seemed to work). I've since dedicated an entire box to terrestrials, expanding the variety, colors, and sizes. Every now and then, I need to dip into my bag of tricks and pull out an odd color or size. However, you don't need to be that elaborate. A few different patterns in a few common sizes will usually do the trick. An exact match isn't critical unless the wind is blowing a fair number of ants, flying ants, hoppers, or whatever onto the water, and the fish are feeding single-mindedly. At times like this, you'll probably need to get near the exact size and color (size being more important), because the take will be selective. Match as closely as you can. If that doesn't work, switch to an entirely different bug or fly. If you get *really* desperate, you could glue a live specimen to a hook and cast it out. I'm just kidding, but I have felt that frustrated.

I realize you can't buy everything at once, so let me suggest a few patterns you ought to carry. This is a generic sort of listing. You may need to modify the list for your home waters or the waters you plan to visit.

Hoppers. Fish gobble up hoppers. The best general colors are dark yellows and tans, but colors vary depending on the locale, so it's a good idea to check before you hit the water. Hoppers are deadly from midsummer to early fall, especially on a windy day. Use fly sizes #6-12. The #8 is the best all-purpose fly. Fish at a dead drift or twitch the hopper as if it were struggling on the surface.

Ants (Flying Ants). Fish devour ants, too—perhaps more eagerly than they eat hoppers. Ants are a fish delicacy that's always in good taste. They are probably your best choice, and are the first terrestrial you should carry in your fly tackle arsenal. The best color is black, next

A few hopper patterns are a must for every fly box.

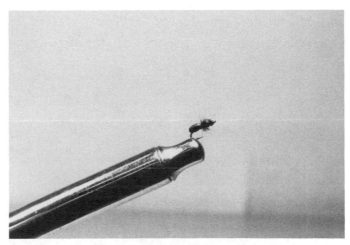

When all else fails, tie on an ant. Keep on hand a selection of ants in different sizes and colors.

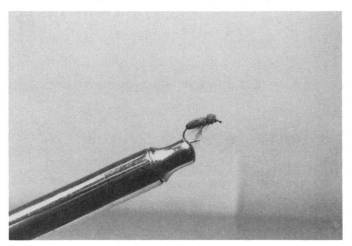

Beetles are a trout delicacy.

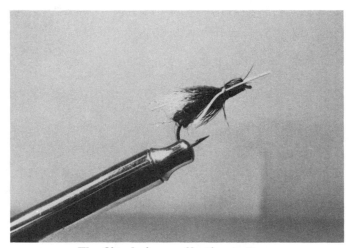

The Cicada is an effective pattern.

This ragged-looking fly is a mouse pattern.

is a blackish brown. The only difference between ants and flying ants is wings. Many casters on a budget carry only flying ants and clip the wings when necessary to match the hatch. For the price of one fly, they have two. For high mountain lakes and streams, ants are a must. They are often the only meals that tempt finicky trout. Use fly sizes #14-18. The #16 is the best all-purpose fly. Fish at a dead drift.

Beetles. Use fly sizes #8-14. The #12 is the best all-purpose fly. The best color, and about the *only* color, is black. Fish at a dead drift.

After you've built a collection of hoppers, ants, and beetles in various sizes and colors, you may want to add a few extra terrestrials, including crickets (#8), cicadas (#4-6), bees, and moths.

Mice. Yes, you just read the word *mice*. Mice aren't insects, but they are food for big trout, and they make an excellent offering for lunkers like monster browns.

I've given you a generic overview of terrestrials. However, there are color variations in different geographic regions, and different waters call for different terrestrials. Overall, the ant is my favorite offering. However, I can think of a half-dozen rivers where cicadas and hoppers are more productive. You have to be sensitive to your water and, in my mind, size is still the most important consideration.

Presentations. It almost goes without saying that you must present your terrestrial correctly. A proper presentation may require a long leader and a light tippet. When you cast your fly, it's okay if you let it *slap* or *plop* on the water—something you wouldn't want to do with a mayfly. A terrestrial hits the drink with a *clunk*.

Ants, beetles, crickets, and other such bugs don't have much buoyancy, so they float low. They ride on the drift, almost in the film, and they're somewhat waterlogged. I like to fish them as close to me as I can. I always wear dark glasses when fishing, so I can track the drift. If you take your eyes off the water for a second, you might miss the rise.

I especially enjoy hunting an aggressive fish and presenting to it. Instead of fishing at the likely spots, I'll take my larger terrestrials and go fish-finding. I spend more time walking, but it's not time wasted.

Why Do They Work? For most fish, terrestrials aren't a main food source—instead, they're a tasty snack. Many fishermen have wondered why fish are so eager to attack a morsel that's atypical. Maybe there is a code in the trout's brain that signals it to go for a hopper, even when it's feeding on something else. Ants seem especially delicious to fish, and the other terrestrials aren't far behind.

Maybe it's a good expenditure of the fish's energy. A hopper or a beetle is a much larger mouthful than a mayfly or a midge. Or perhaps it's a conditioned response—a case of the fish jumping at good fortune just as we might snatch hundred-dollar bills floating in the air above our heads. It may not have happened to us before. Indeed, we may never have thought about it. Still, when it happens, we jump at the money.

Or maybe fewer fly fishers throw terrestrials, so the fish haven't learned to be wary of them. For whatever reason, terrestrials work, and work well. Using them is a great way to catch fish.

A GROUP OF YELLOWSTONE RAINBOWS FLY CAST WITH A COUNTERFEIT TWENTY DOLLAR BILL.

SCHOOL

EIGHT

A Handful of Magic
Basic Patterns and Essential Attractors

THERE ARE A ZILLION FLIES, and it's hard to know where to start. If I might generalize, flies can be imitating patterns, attractor patterns, or both.

For someone just learning the sport of fly fishing, casting alone isn't enough. Besides getting the right fly, there's staying out of the drink, avoiding slippery rocks, selecting the right leader, trying not to throw a shadow in a likely pool, and more. Thank heaven for attractors!

There are flies that perform a certain function, imitating a specific bug. Casters use them when they're matching the hatch, because these are specific patterns tied to look like specific bugs.

There are other flies called *attractors*. These are patterns that have proven very effective. In fact, you could do well fishing attractors for the rest of your life and ignoring specifics entirely. Attractors don't look like any specific food, but they still attract fish.

A trout will often take an attractor with a vengeance. Notice how the caster lifts the rod to keep the line taut. You can't allow a slack line if you want to land your fish.

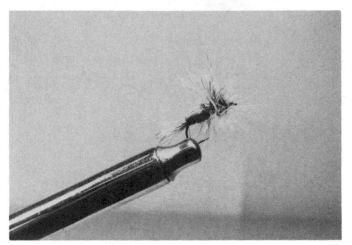

The Humpy is a very popular attractor pattern.

Why Do Attractors Work?

If you figure it out, give me a collect call. I'm not really sure why attractor patterns work. I've never interviewed a trout, so what I'm going to tell you is my best guess.

Attractors imitate life. They look "buglike" in a general sense. They represent something that looks familiar in a generic way. Perhaps an attractor works on a fish the same way a new dish does on a human. Maybe you've never tried a certain dish, but if it looks good when you see it for the first time, you're likely to dive in.

Using attractors is an easy and effective way to start catching fish while you're learning the subtle and sometimes frustrating points of matching the hatch. Let's take a look at some of the attractor patterns you'll want to collect for your fly box. For the time being, this will provide you with everything you need to fish effectively. In fact, there are millions of successful fly casters who have used nothing but a handful of attractors. If you're armed with

seven dry attractor patterns and six wet attractor patterns, you will be prepared to take on just about any water.

One night after a great day of casting, we got on the subject of attractors and came up with a list. I've listed what we came up with, as well as recommended sizes. I've also indicated the best ways to fish each fly. Some of the patterns we suggest work as specific patterns, too. We could call them crossovers.

Best Attractor Dry Fly Patterns

Adams: fly sizes #14-20. #16 is the best all-purpose.
Fish in a dead drift. This is the best all-around dry pattern. It's at the top of nearly everyone's list. It was originally tied to imitate a caddis, but it seems to mimic just about everything effectively. When in doubt, tie on an Adams. You can use it for a mayfly, a caddis, or a midge (in small sizes).

Elk Hair Caddis: fly sizes #14-18. #16 is the best all-purpose.
Fish in a dead drift, or twitch the fly slightly as you take in the line. This is obviously caddis-specific, but it also works as a general pattern. I've even used it to represent a dun.

Royal Wulff: fly sizes #12-16. #14 is the best all-purpose.
Fish in a dead drift. This fly imitates life, and it seems to imitate a generic terrestrial. It floats quite well.

Goofus Bug: sizes #12-16. #16 is the best all-purpose.

Fish in a dead drift. This fly can be used to represent a caddis or a terrestrial—or just about anything else.

Renegade: sizes #14-20. #16 and #20 are the best all-purpose.

Fish in a dead drift, twitch the fly slightly, retrieve, and strip (pull in the line with quick movements). This fly represents "bug" in general. In the small sizes, meaning #18 and espe-cially #20, it can be used to imitate a midge or a small fly.

Griffith's Gnat: sizes #18-22. #20 is the best all-purpose.

Fish in a dead drift. This little bugger works really well, and it's a good general midge imitation.

Mosquito: sizes #16-20. #18 is the best all-purpose.

Fish in a dead drift. Most mosquito patterns are pretty generic. This is a good general fly.

The Royal Wulff is one of the most beloved and successful attractors around.

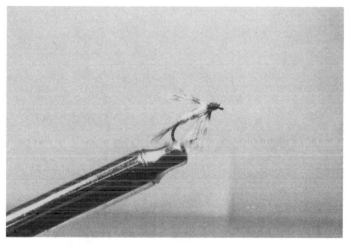
The Gray Hackle Yellow, a wet pattern.

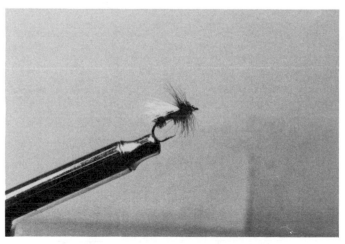
This fly is a take-off on the Royal Wulff.

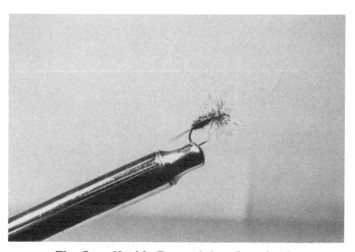
The Gray Hackle Peacock is a favorite fly.

Other good choices might include the *Coachman* (or *Royal Coachman*) and the *Gray Hackle Yellow.* The Coachman-type fly is similar to the Royal Wulff and can be fished the same way. I like it a lot, but it doesn't ride in the water quite as well as the Wulff. When I was 16 years old, I fished a modified Coachman for a solid year—wet and dry. I still use a #18 and a #20 on high mountain lakes.

Best Attractor Wet Fly Patterns

Hare's Ear: sizes #14-18. #16 is the best all-purpose.
Fish in a dead drift or with an occasional twitch. In my mind, this is the best wet fly nymph. It's good for everything. It can pass for a caddis, a stone fly, or a mayfly nymph.

Pheasant Tail: sizes #16-20. #18 is the best all-purpose.
Fish in a dead drift. Here's the second-best attractor pattern. It can pass for a mayfly nymph, a midge larva, and general food.

Prince Nymph: sizes #12-16. #14 is the best all-purpose.
Fish in a dead drift. This is a great general bug pattern. It works well as a catch-all fly.

Woolly Bugger or *Woolly Worm:* sizes #6-12. #8 is the best all-purpose.
Fish in a dead drift, twitch, strip, jig, and jerk (strong, hard pulls on the line). This pattern can pass for a leech, a minnow, or a general bug.

Muddler Minnow: sizes #6-10. #8 is the best all-purpose.
Fish in a dead drift, twitch, strip, hop, jig, and bounce. This is a great generic fry (juvenile fish) imitation. It represents small prey.

Serendipity: sizes #16-20. #20 is the best all-purpose.
Fish in a dead drift.

Later you'll want to use more specific flies. For the time being, however, you'll catch quite a few fish with attractor patterns. I recommend that you collect the "all-purpose" size first. Then add other sizes as your budget allows.

**The Woolly Worm is a
popular and effective pattern.**

READ THE WATER LIKE A BOOK

NINE

Reading the Water

Thinking Like a Fish

EVEN IF YOU HAVE THE PERFECTLY TIED FLY and the right line, rod, reel, and leader, you're in trouble if you can't read the water. You might as well fish in mud puddles. This chapter will teach you to think like a fish so you'll do more hooking and less casting. It will cover essential fish lore, how fish feed, and where they hold (or stay). The chapter will also discuss how to approach the water, and the basic techniques for working different kinds of water.

Fishing is one of those wonderful sports in which you sometimes get lucky even if you do everything wrong. However, if you want to hook fish consistently, you have to do a lot of things right. You can have the most expensive custom rod in the world. You can have the best reel and fly line. You can have the best fly a craftsman can tie. You can look like you just stepped out of an L.L. Bean, Eddie Bauer, Dunn's, or Cabella's catalog. But as my saintly father used to say, "Michael, my boy, all the extras ain't worth crap if ya ain't catchin' fish 'cause yer fishing where there ain't none." Dad was a country doctor. I assume he was quot-

Fishing at dawn is a great delight. This small peninsula is a good place to start casting.

101

Decide where you're going to stand before you crash into the water. A careful caster will not walk through water that might hold fish.

ing one of his patients. He spouted this quote when we fished, and he repeated it when we hunted blacktail deer in the fall. But he had a point, and his point brings me to mine. You've got to fish where the fish are.

That point was graphically illustrated to me several autumns ago on the Yellowstone River. I was photographing bears, and I wisely hadn't brought along my rod. If I had, I wouldn't have completed my photographic work.

My blind was several hundred yards from the road, overlooking an elk carcass. Several days earlier, a young bull had been hit by a yellow tour bus and had managed to stumble off the road before dying. A sow grizzly and her cub had been feeding off the windfall. I hoped to catch the pair breakfasting, so I could snap a few frames. I was in my blind from dawn to dusk, hoping they'd get hungry and feed during the day.

At the same time, I happened to have a perfect view of the river and the fly casters.

While waiting for bears I studied the anglers through my powerful binoculars. There wasn't much else to do. I glanced at the bull, watched the casters, glanced at the bull, and watched the casters. You get the idea. Anyway, after dawn, the parking areas filled up. Lots of perfectly dressed folks with expensive fishing gear poured out of their vehicles.

As the small herd of fly fishers hoofed down to the water, I noticed something curious. There was plenty of river, so no one had to crowd or fight for a place to stand. About half of them just plunged into the water in their high-tech gear and started casting. The other half weren't as anxious. These folks studied the water for a time, maybe crawling up on a bank to survey the current. After a few minutes of examining, they finally jumped in the cold water, wearing and carrying the same sort of gear. Because I was bored and wanted to join them, I made mental notes of where everyone was fishing. I decided to check their progress throughout the morning. I glanced at the dead elk for a while, then turned back to the Yellowstone River.

Before too long, guess what? Many of those who plunged into the river and fished without a lick of forethought weren't doing too well. They were catching a few fish, but not many. On the other hand, not so far away—sometimes just a few yards away—other fly fishers were hooking a fish every few casts.

There wasn't a lack of fish. Cutthroat trout were popping out of the water. Most of the anglers had top-notch gear. Why were some casters catching fish consistently, while others weren't?

Because some were fishing the wrong part of the river. You have to fish to the fish. All the gear in the world won't help if you don't throw your flies where the fish are.

You must read the water like a book.

Reading the Water

What do we mean by "reading the water"? You can't really read it like a book, can you?

The difference between the person catching fish and the person not catching fish is often the water they fish. This might sound stupid, but you have to think like a fish. Remember, fish have a brain about the size of a pea, yet they seem to outsmart us on a regular basis.

Maybe *outsmart* is the wrong term. It's not so much that fish outsmart us, but that we are ignorant of their fishy lifestyle: where they feed, when they feed, how they feed; when they are aggressive or neutral; what types of water they like; and how they breed. All these things are important. When you fish, you must make a number of conscious choices before you tie on a fly or select a place to fish.

Reading the water means looking at a stretch of stream and deciding how you're going to fish it. Where would you start if you were going to fish this water? Look for boulders and snags. Look for seams where two currents come together.

When you look at a given patch of water, ask yourself where you would be if you were a fish. What you are doing is cutting the variables. You aren't fishing randomly any longer. Instead, you are fishing by design.

Remember three things:

1. Fish actively feeding are called aggressive.
2. Fish feeding specifically on one kind of food are called selective.
3. Fish resting or feeding randomly are called neutral.

Aggressive Fish. When you pray at night, always ask that the fish will be aggressive, not just hungry. Aggressive fish make the sport fun, because you can't do much wrong if you get a fly in their general vicinity. They take a little of the challenge out of a flawless cast or perfectly matching the hatch, but after a few frustrating days when nothing seems to work, aggressive fish are great for your ego. It won't matter if your presentation is off, if you flog the water, or if your shadow creeps over the fish. An aggressive trout (or bass, walleye, or bluegill) will hit anything, and hit it hard.

Trout taking anything on or in the water—boiling on the surface—make a shark feeding frenzy look tame. When fish get like this, it goes beyond hunger. It's an obsession. The fish stand in line, fighting each other for the privilege of taking your fly and even knocking each other out of the way to get it. Cherish the moment. It only happens now and then, when something in nature seems to make all trout go berserk. A fish that would previously wait for a #26 fly per-

Before you hit the water, take stock of your flies, making sure you have patterns that match the hatch.

fectly timed, presented, and tied will now hit a bare catfish hook.

Selective Fish. Finicky eaters, these. Selective fish are better than nothing, but they're often hard to catch. They are feeding on a specific hatch, and that's about all they'll take. An odd attractor pattern might provoke a hit now and then, but as a rule, when fish are selective it's time to dig into your fly box and match the hatch.

Selective fish are so focused on eating just one thing that they seem to ignore almost everything else. Even a nice juicy night crawler wouldn't turn their finicky heads. Their feeding response is tuned into a certain hatch, so you need to present a fly pattern that looks exactly like what they're lunching on.

Besides hoping they turn aggressive, the best course of action is trying to match the size. As I've said before, the fly size you select is probably more important than the color or pattern. Ideally you want the exact pattern and the exact size, but it's not always possible. You settle for what you have in your fly box or what you can beg, borrow, or steal.

Neutral Fish. Neutral fish don't seem hungry. Generally they're resting. They're very fishable, but you have to go to them. Most fly casters tell stories about dropping a fly and watching a fish travel 10 or 20 feet to gobble it up. This happens only with aggressive fish. Neutral fish are laid back. They might move an inch or two.

If you want them to pick up your presentation, you must drift your fly right in front of their noses. If a presentation looks tasty and very easy, they'll sometimes take it, but they won't expend any energy to do so. Neutral fish are finicky, but not because they're being selective. They just aren't very hungry. Attractor patterns often work well on these fish. My favorite tempters of neutral fish are an Adams or a Coachman pattern for dry flies; the Pheasant Tail and the Hare's Ear for wet flies.

Truthfully, though, I'm not sure if it really matters *what* you throw at them. What's more important is having a perfect drift without drag and floating the fly within an inch or so of the fish's mouth. Ideally, you don't want the fish to have to do more than open its mouth—or at the most, turn its head.

Thinking Like a Fish

When you think like a fish, there won't be a lot on your mind. You'll want an easy life—all the food you can gobble without effort, crea-

Don't overlook moss lines, the fish's pantry. They're excellent places to fish.

ture comforts, color TV, someone to deliver your welfare check. As a fish you're phlegmatic and moody. You're lazy, because all fish are lazy. But once a year, all this changes. You think about sex. But the thought doesn't last. After a few weeks of madness, you're back to normal.

Maybe putting fish and *thinking* together isn't right. Fish don't think. They respond. So as a fish, what would you normally be preoccupied with? Food, personal comfort, and safety.

Food: A fish will spend most of its life looking for food that can be eaten without expending energy. Ideally, a fish wants to locate itself in a spot where the drift will bring breakfast, but where it won't have to move far or expend much energy fighting the current. A fish will eat aquatic and terrestrial insects in various stages of development, crustaceans, and other fish.

Personal Comfort: A fish will strive for a spot in the water where it doesn't have to fight the current. It also seeks water that is the right temperature and has enough oxygen. Constantly fighting the current burns too much energy. Thus, a fish will stay behind a rock or some other structure to break up the flow. A fish needs water of a certain temperature—colder or warmer water can be stressful and depleted of oxygen. If a fish can find food where its personal comforts are met, that's where it will be. If not, it will travel in the water to feed, but it will return to a comfort zone when lunch is over.

Safety: Most fish never make it. The odds that a fish will live from egg to adult are one in tens of thousands. Throughout its life, a fish is understandably paranoid about its safety and is constantly looking over its fins. Danger is an ever-present factor, and it's the reason why fish spook easily. Fish like to hide. They seek the safety of deep water, moss, the shadows of overhanging banks, or structure. However, a fish often has to leave safe water to feed, and it may stay away as long as the feeding is good. But it will always retreat to what it considers safe water. As a fry and then as a small fish, it always had to contend with larger fish and other predators that were trying to munch on it. As it grew larger, it faced danger from the air (raptors) and from mammalian predators. Only the toughest, luckiest fish reach even a modest size.

Types of Water

Whether you're fishing in streams, lakes, or ponds, a fish's needs are the same. Because you'll be casting most of the time in streams, and because streams are diversified, I'll spend a little more time discussing techniques for fishing flowing water.

Different types of water in a stream help fish meet their three basic needs. A stream can be roughly divided into four divisions: smooth (flat) water, pools, glide water (runs), and choppy water (riffles). As you approach a

When you're fishing a lake or pond, look for a rock outcrop, a place fish naturally cruise for food.

stream, you have several things to consider. Where do you start? Nothing is popping on the water, so where do you throw your line? In the smooth water, the pools, or the choppy water? What's best? Let's look at each type of water.

Where's the best water? Being armed with a fine cast, a good line, and a fine collection of flies ain't enough. This is partly what we mean by reading the water. Look at the water and know where to start—don't start at any old place by default. Trout move to different parts of the water as needs change, as the season changes, and as the weather changes.

Smooth (Flat) Water. Smooth, flat water is fun to fish. The relatively smooth bottoms manifest themselves in an even surface. Smooths are nice wading. They're from one to five feet deep, and they often hold a good supply of food. The water is comfortable, but it is not secure—especially in the shallow sections.

Look for fish along banks and undercuts, where two currents meet, where a creek enters, in shadows, and on the edges of moss lines. The advantage is food; hatches are concentrated in those areas. Fish will try to feed near a zone of safety, staying in the feeding lane when the food is heavy and moving back to safety when the hatch slackens. Look for places a fish can hide. Look for *lines* or *seams*. These are places where two types of water meet—riffles, moss, drop-offs, deep and shallow.

Watch the water. Can you see the fish? If possible, stand on a piece of high ground and look. Can you see the fish feeding in the water? If you see fish near the surface, what else do you see? The judgments you make are important. Just because you see signs of fish activity doesn't mean a dry fly is in order. Fishing the wrong fly will improve your casting skills, but it won't produce many fish.

Sometimes reading the water means wading from bank to bank.

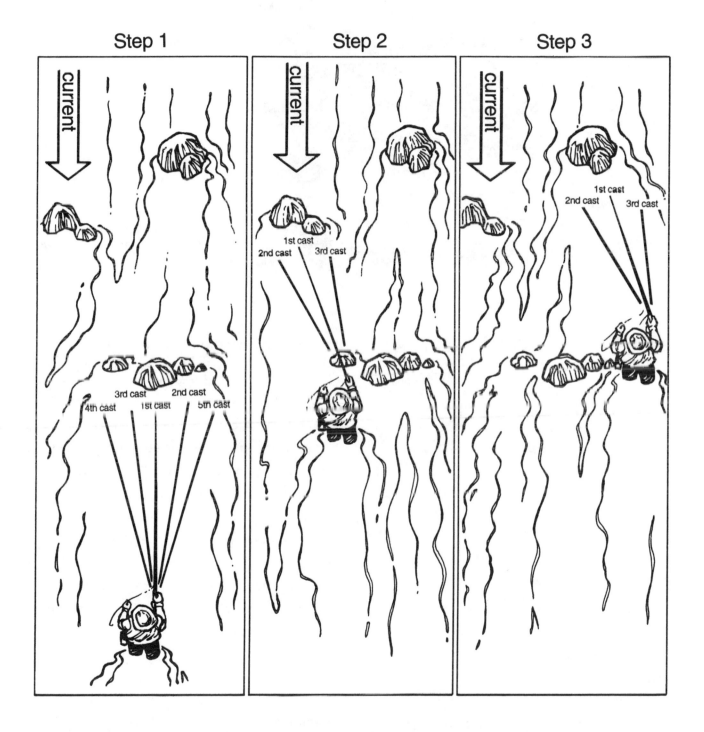

Read the water and plan your moves. Try working the eddy pools behind rocks and the seams where fast water meets slower water. After fishing one pool, move upstream to the next. (The numbers refer to the order of the casts.)

All of this water looks alike. Check carefully for fallen logs or boulders, where fish might hide.

Look for:

Head and Tail Activity. This tells you the fish are feeding just under the surface, probably on some type of emerger.

Gulping or Ringing Activity. This tells you the fish are feeding right on the film. You'll see a delicate ring or bubble on the water, a gulping, or a sipping. You won't see the fish's body.

If you see heads and tails, fish emerger patterns just below the film. If you see gulping, go with a dry fly. Observe what the hatch is, and try to match it with your fly.

Pools of Water. The water is deep and slow. The biggest fish usually call this patch of water home, because they've monopolized the best lanes and feeding zones. It's best to fish pools in the early morning and later evening.

Pools are excellent places to fish large patterns and streamers. Food often comes in big sizes, and fish are accustomed to eating fry,

leeches, sculpin, and crayfish. Crayfish and Muddler patterns are good choices here.

Glide Water (Runs). The surface is partially smooth, but the bottom of the river is broken up with large boulders and structure. The current isn't fast, but it's frequently powerful. The water is wadable and about 2½ to 7 feet deep. Because it's deep, you often can't see the fish. You have to look at the surface of the water and try to figure out where to the fish will be concentrated. Because the bottom is broken up by structure, the fish can stay comfortably on the bottom and wait for drifting food.

Again look for edges—for places where two different currents meet, for a creek mouth, a moss line, or anything that breaks the current. In these spots, fish find food and relief from the current. Unless there is a good hatch on, you'll have to get down deep to the fish. A dry fly isn't the answer. Fish a nymph on a dead drift, using enough shot (or weighted line) to get the imitation down. You'll usually want to place it just above the bottom, but you'll have to experiment. Mending will be critical. When all else fails, try a terrestrial pattern like a hopper.

This may not be the best "food water," but it's comfortable and safe. Fish will be opportunistic in their feeding habits.

Choppy Water (Riffles). Fast water isn't deep. A fish comes here to feed. This is a feeding zone, so you'll find hungry fish here. The water probably won't be comfortable or safe. The surface is choppy, and the bottom is rough. While the water may seem very swift, remem-

ber that the bottom is broken up with structure. There are plenty of places a fish can use to escape the current while it's in a feeding lane.

When you're fishing the chop, you can't take any water for granted, because fish will be scattered all over. Depending on the needs of the day, you can fish the film with dry flies, use emergers, or fish the bottom. Because the water is choppy, you can get fairly close to fish without being seen.

No matter where you're fishing, look for places where a fish might hold, then present your fly. Work all sections of the stream quickly, paying special attention to edges and underwater structure.

Before you know it, you'll be thinking like a fish.

Sometimes reading the water means walking to a good area.
Notice the rocks in the middle of the river—they're worth checking out.

THIS FISH HAD BEEN CAUGHT AND RELEASED SO MANY TIMES THAT IT HAD LEARNED TO STEAL WATCHES.

TEN

Put 'Em Back Alive
Catch and Release

THE CONSUMPTIVE MENTALITY IS BAGGAGE LEFT OVER FROM OUR FRONTIER DAYS. It was tough to make a go of it on our rugged frontier. You took what food you could, when you could. It was harsh, but there seemed to be an endless supply. The buffalo, the grizzly, the wolf, the passenger pigeon, the elk, the antelope, and the deer were all victims. It was all take, take, take, with little thought of tomorrow. If you clear-cut a forest, overgrazed a tract of land, or polluted a stream, you moved on. For a while, at least, there was always somewhere else to move on to. We got the idea that we could take and never replace.

In the glory days of a famous trout lake named Strawberry in my part of the Rockies, it seemed that everyone caught monster trout for years and years. For many families, pulling the trailer up to the 'Berry and sending the men out in a boat to slay liberal limits of trout was at least an annual affair. Smiling anglers came back with their mighty catches, handing the big fish over to the womenfolk. While the ladies canned the fish, the men went out on the water again to "harvest" more lunkers. After a couple of days,

and with enough canned fish to last Napoleon's Army halfway to Moscow, the departing family felt all warm and fuzzy as they drove down the mountain. Another group slid into their camping place as they pulled out. The process began again.

Is it any wonder that it all ran out?

After a while, frustrated anglers began to say, "Where in the heck are all the fish?" Obviously, the fish were in the finest fruit cellars along the Wasatch Front, next to the blue-ribbon bread-and-butter pickles and the extra-sugary cling peaches.

"It ain't like it used to be," an old-timer who happened to be my friend's grandfather used to say, rolling the quid in his beard-rough cheek before he thoughtfully spit. "Them days is gone forever. Why, I used to see a time when you could catch ye a load by Indian Creek . . ."

Yes, those days of consumption are gone, but good fishing can be around for a long time. In all fairness, other factors besides too much taking affected Strawberry Lake, but it peaked more quickly than was necessary. Fish were viewed as an inexhaustible food source, but this attitude is slowly changing.

Catchin' Fish. If it's not obvious by now, I love to catch fish. I also love to eat fish. Nothing is more delicious than a tasty fish fry or a slowly grilled fillet. Picture this: A group of fly fishing buddies, gorged to the gills on tender, slightly pink trout steaks, raise their half-drained glasses of frosty root beer to the day's adventure, to good friends, and to the big ones that got away, unashamedly lying through their teeth. The 14-inch fish have become 18- or 20-inch fish, and that really big one might have gone nine pounds.

The reality is somewhat different. Among all anglers, fly fishers are traditionally the most ecological and the most likely to hook and let live. Before anyone else, fly casters started to preach catch and release. That brings me to the question: Can fly casters eat fish? Do they dare? Must they turn in their rods if they do?

A number of my friends claim they've never killed a fish (on purpose, at least). There's little moderation on either side of the fish-killing question these days.

Let's take a look at the history of catching fish. We were once a "put and take" country. Hatcheries worked overtime, cranking out fry to keep the worm drowners and cheese floaters in their limits of small, flabby trout that seemed

A fly fisher in action, preparing to release a good-sized trout.

to eat anything. However, the face of fishing has changed. There are now about ten zillion more anglers than there were when I was in knickers. Many rivers are cesspools, and others are now unfishable. State and federal hatchery budgets have been slashed. Here's the bottom line: More fishers means less productive water, more pressure, and restrictive catch limits. The emphasis on fishing has gone from consumption to recreation. There are fewer fish to eat, but we still have the fun of catching them. Today we're more concerned with the art of catching and less concerned with keeping.

Fly casting is the solution, not the problem. The nature of our sport is one of technique and skill. It's hard to release a fish that's been snared on a chrome-plated, spring-loaded, three-barbed, razor-honed, custom-made, proud as punch "Seagull Paw" cheese hook. But many of us know that fish are a renewable resource that we can enjoy again and again.

The word is getting out that fish can be caught repeatedly. We are making progress, but the word isn't all the way out yet. As I suggested earlier, camps have fallen into two extremes. There are still too many who would rather part with a thumb or some other favorite organ than let a fish swim away after they've hooked it. Perhaps it's some sort of perfidious manhood thing. Do lots of dead fish equal one big man?

In my opinion, nearly all the fish you catch ought to be released. You'll be catching so many that it's the only legal way you can continue to cast. Besides, it's a good, snobbish habit to get into. After hooking a nice fish and doing battle, it's a swell feeling to let it go so you can match wits with it another day. The put and take angler hits the water, gets a limit, and goes home. For the fly caster, it's a process. Why catch a few fish, then go home to dirty garages and shaggy lawns? It's better to catch fish all day. The legal limit would be limiting, so you let 'em go and keep casting flies.

But despite all this soapbox preaching, don't feel it's morally wrong to take a few fish now and then. The key word is *few*—and only now and then. Some casters vehemently insist that you should never slay a fish. Personally, I release most everything, but I keep a few with a clear conscience. Not all the fish you catch are equal. Here's what I think about before I take a fish home for eating:

I never keep a fish from a catch and release water.

I never keep a fish from water that receives high fishing pressure.

When I kill fish, I take only enough for one meal, not a supply to fill the freezer.

I let the native fish swim and keep the planters. I let the 19-inch trout go but keep the 12-inch planter for the pan.

I have a high minimum standard for the fish I keep as wall hangers.

Taking a few "eaters" or one for the wall once in a while is okay. I personally haven't had a fish mounted yet, but I swear I'm going to one of these days. I try to shy away from the fish that are optimum breeding size, because I want them out obeying their impulses.

You have to know your water. In some water, pulling out a few nice fish might be a sin, because it would negatively impact the ecosystem. In other waters, it may actually help—or at least have little or no impact. Do what's right for the water. If you keep this in mind, you won't go wrong.

As a result of strict creel limits and catch and release, many waters have been saved or improved. Can you imagine what would happen if casters were allowed to keep cutthroat on the Yellowstone River in Yellowstone National Park? Thousands and thousands of anglers enjoy the water every year, because of catch and release. The story goes on.

Proving You Caught 'Em

You decide you want to let that really, really big fish go. It fought the good fight, and it ought to be heading back to the bottom of the drink. Still, you've lied so much in the past that no one will ever believe you caught it. You've stretched the truth 40 times. You've been caught transforming a minnow into Moby Dick. Remember it's okay to lie, your state fishing license gives you that right. However, before you get the art of fishing fibbery down, you'll get caught in your own snare a few times. Now you've finally caught a monster. The truth is better than the fictions you've invented, but who

AS A COURTESY,
OFFER FISH A COPY OF THE
PHOTO BEFORE RELEASE.

will believe you? Yet you'd like to let that fish go. It's a serious problem.

The solution? Carry a camera in your vest or pack. If you're with a buddy, ask him or her to snap off a few shots and witness the lunker. Fishing buddies are always willing to work with you on a few camera angles, because you'd do the same for them.

Hints for Good Shots. Make sure the sun is at the photographer's back, and watch to see that your shadow doesn't get in the way. Don't forget that the bill of your hat will cause a shadow on your face. Since you probably won't be using your camera's filler flash, tilt the hat up, twist it so the bill is in the back, or take it off. Try not to take a direct, head-on shot. Kneel down and shoot up; climb on a bank and shoot down; or have the subject kneel down in the water. This will help you keep the fish healthier, too. Keep the fish nice and shiny-wet. Water dripping off the fish is a nice touch.

Don't keep the fish out too long, but try to shoot from several different angles to ensure good composition and the right light. Bracket a stop up and a stop down from the suggested exposure, because light and water can play

The best way to capture a trophy is to have a friend record it on film. Make sure your buddy takes shots from different angles.

I took this shot while holding the camera in one hand and the fish in the other.

tricks on camera meters. A polarizing filter, which is like sunglasses for your camera, will help you take the guesswork out of reflection.

A good 35 mm "point and shoot" camera is the easiest to use, because you won't have to fumble with f-stops and other settings. You can simply put the dot on someone's chest and shoot, but taking pictures from several angles is necessary to ensure a good shot. You'll get better shots with a more traditional camera, but you might have to preset it, and you'll probably have to show your buddy how to use it. There are a number of good point and shoot cameras for the caster to choose

from. I use a waterproof camera and always carry it in a Ziploc plastic bag inside of a foam case. I've been known to slip and fall even in the best of situations, taking an icy bath the hard way. My cameras have survived better than I have.

A good photo is worth 10,000 words or a wonderfully crafted fishing lie. There is no doubt about the results of your casting. Plus, if you have the right telephoto lens, you can add 10 to 20 percent to the size your fish.

Taking Photos When You're Alone. If your luck is like mine, you'll catch the biggest fish of your life when you're alone. There's no one to see it and collaborate. What do you do? Take a picture of yourself, of course. You can do it, but it's not easy. It's hard to set up a tripod, keep the fish healthy, and compose the shot in one fell swoop. It's a massive coordinating effort.

I usually don't try to get myself in the photo when I'm alone—just my trophy. First, I head to the shallows. I keep the fish at bay and the tension on the line while I fumble for the camera and adjust it to get as much shutter speed as I can with a medium depth of field. I like to shoot fish next to my rod and around the rocks, if possible. I snap off a few shots and let the lunker go. If there are big boulders nearby, I might set my camera on one and use the timer. When I've had the right lens on the camera, I've been known to hold the fish at arm's length or in the net and fire off some shots.

Live Mounting. You've hooked your dream fish. You'd like the thing stuffed, but you can't abide the idea of killing him. You know he'd look really swell on the mantle next to your wife's trophy elk and the porcelain China dolls. What do you do?

It's called a live mount. Measure the fish from nose to tail. Measure the girth. Take a color picture. Armed with this data, there are a number of mighty fine taxidermists who can make an exact replica, or live mount. It's a nice way to go. You have a replica of your trophy for the drawing room, yet the real fish is still around, making baby fish and perpetuating its superior genetic strain.

How to Catch and Release

Not too long ago, I was catching fish at Electric Lake in the Manti Mountains in central Utah. I'd like to think it was due to my brilliant cast and superb technique, but *everyone* was catching fish that day. No one could do anything wrong. The fly casters and spinners were bringing in pan-sized trout with every other cast. Since the water was catch and release, all the fish were being let go. But tragically, many fish would never live to the end of the month—and it was August 30. There were dead fish on the shore as a sad testimony. All had been released. Some of the fish I caught had patches of fungus growing on them because improper handling had removed the protective slime. Improper catch and release should be called "catch and die later." Fish don't have a prayer if they aren't released properly. But they're a renewable resource if you do it right. Here's how:

1. *Don't wear the fish out.* Fish that you release can still die. Certain chemical changes take place when a fish is played to exhaustion. Bring your fish in as quickly as possible, and avoid the temptation to overplay.

2. *Wet your hands before you touch your fish.* Dry hands remove some of the film on the fish. This fishy slime or mucus protects a fish against infections.

3. *Don't squish the fish or finger the gills.* Fish wiggle like hell, but you can't squish them to get the hook out.

Don't touch the eyes, either. Be gentle. Remember that you can catch this fish again.

4. *Keep the fish in the water.* Most of the time, you can release a fish while it's still in the water. With a little practice, you can hold the hook with your finger or a hemostat and slide it out easily.

5. *Cut the leader if the hook is in too deeply.* Lose a fly, save a fish. If the fly is in the mouth or throat, or imbedded in the flesh, cut the leader. The natural liquids in the fish will completely erode the metal in a short time. The fish will be just fine.

6. *Hold the fish up in the water.* You do the best you can, but sometimes the fish is tired. Let it rest. Hold it up gently, suspended in the water. In a moment, after it has rested, it will take off.

7. *Respirate if necessary.* On occasion, you might need to move the fish back and forth through the water. This gets water moving through its gills, so more oxygen can be absorbed. It's called respirating the fish. Hold the fish gently. As soon as it can, it will scoot for cover.

To ensure that your fish swims off safely, you may have to hold it by the tail and move it gently back and forth to get water moving through its gills. If the fish is exhausted, hold it in the water until it swims off under its own power.

ELEVEN

About the Trout

Hooking Browns, 'Bows, Brooks, and Cuts

ONCE, WHEN I WAS CASTING FLIES FOR CUTTHROAT TROUT ON THE BEAR RIVER IN WYOMING, my buddy Gary told me a fascinating story about the creation of the world. I assume it's true, and I'd like to share it with you:

> In the beginning, God made the heavens and the earth. But that wasn't enough, so He made the streams, the rivers, the lakes, and the mighty seas. For his sacred gift to man, He made the trout. But one kind of trout, He decided, simply wasn't enough. So He made many trout.
>
> He made the German brown, the smartest trout in the water.
>
> He made the rainbow, the greatest leaping trout in the water.
>
> He made the brook, the most beautiful trout in the water.
>
> He made the cutthroat, the dumbest trout in the water.
>
> Then He commanded his elect to go forth and fish mightily with flies and to treat his gift with great respect.

When someone mentions trout, I get cold shivers of excitement. I'm now 38 years old, and I hope I'll never outgrow the thrill. Whenever I see a stretch of water larger than a mud puddle, I feel the way I did when I was a kid. I want to grab my rod and fish. I caught my first official wild trout, a rainbow, at Four-Bit Creek in southern Oregon. I was with my dad, and I was five years old. I caught the fish on a small, gold salmon-egg hook with a piece of red yarn. This was my first fly fishing experience. My dad made me a willow fly rod, and I fished for several blissful days.

Two waters diverged in a yellow wood. I picked the blue-ribbon trout stream, and that has made all the difference. Trout are the number one quarry of the fly caster. Let's learn more about them, because knowledge of our honored prey is power.

Catching Trophy Trout

I suppose the term *trophy* is somewhat relative. On some streams, a one- to two-pound fish would be considered a monster. On other waters, it would be considered a good fish, but nothing to write home about. If I were fishing for cuts on the Bear River, a four-pound fish would be extraordinary. If I were fishing on Pyramid Lake, where the cuts grow large, I'd be pleased with a five-pounder, but not overjoyed. I'd know there were fish in the 30- to 50-pound range out there waiting for me.

Have you ever wondered how fish and game officials estimate the number of fish that inhabit a stretch of water? A team wades up the river with electric nets, shocking fish. The stunned fish are put in a tube, counted, and released.

The term *trophy fish* means a large fish for the water you're fishing—one you'd want to hang on your wall. To catch trophy trout, you have to do quite a few things, if not everything, right. There are some obvious common denominators when you're fishing for trophies. The most important one is this: You must fish where there are trophy fish. You can't catch trophies if you're fishing a water that has none.

Do your homework. Look in the record books, and see where big fish have been caught. How long ago were they caught? In Utah, the record book suggests that a 26-pound cut was caught at Strawberry Reservoir. But if you investigate further, you'll discover that it was caught in the 1930s. The lake no longer holds fish of that size. So do your homework, and focus on proven waters.

Read sporting and fishing magazines to find out about the latest hot spots. If you want to catch a big brown out of a river, for example, you might check current periodicals. You might be advised to pull your trailer to the White River in Arkansas, where large browns are a proven commodity. But knowing that the White River holds big browns isn't enough. You'll also need to know the best places on the water and the best times to fish. If you're looking for hot spots close to home, talk to local trophy anglers.

To catch the hugest fish, you'll often concentrate on lakes, where the trout grow big. If you can, time your efforts to correspond to the spawn, which is especially important when you're dealing with trophy-sized game fish. The spawn will often draw fish into a small area where you can establish an effective fishing focus. Good common "fish sense" goes out the window during the spawn, so you have more of an advantage. For big fish, fish in the right water, at the right time of the year, and in the right *section* of the water.

There are other things you must do. You have to sneak up on the fish, so they don't know you're there. You have to watch your shadow. You have to present the fly in a size and pattern that's acceptable. You must not let your fly drag on the water. And you must read the water correctly, so you're fishing where the big fish are.

Characteristics of Trout

We have been blessed. There are over 100 subspecies of trout in the world. Several dozen species or subspecies live in the United States. The huchen trout, found in Europe and Siberia, is the largest. This monster can weigh over 100 pounds, making it a veritable Jaws. The smallest species of trout lives in Austria and reaches a whopping five inches. As you might expect, all trout have basic similarities. But there are differences, too, some of which are very subtle.

Brown Trout. The German brown is the smartest trout, and for all true anglers, it holds a place of honor. On second thought, we ought to substitute the word *wary* for smart. The brown is the consummate hog of the stream,

but it's also a very finicky eater. It's the most likely of all the trout to turn down live bait with a hook in it. It's likely to turn down a perfectly tied fly, too.

You have to outsmart this fish. You have to consciously pit yourself against the foe. You have to think like the fish. You must know how the fish moves and reacts, so you can anticipate its actions. Here's a Rutter postulate I stole from Gary: For every ounce a brown trout puts on over two pounds, it gets 10 times smarter.

In 1883, a German aristocrat named Baron von Behr sent 100,000 brown trout eggs to Fred Mather, a fisherman and fish hatchery aficionado. Some of these precious eggs were brooded in New York; others were carefully sent by train to Michigan. The experiment was very successful. The Pere Marquette River in Michigan became the first brown-trout stream in the country. New York became the second state to host these fish. Browns have since found a permanent home in most of the United States and southern Canada. As a point of interest, the word *streamline* was coined by the English angler/physicist Sir George Cayley, because of the brown's aerodynamic shape. When he couldn't *catch* the fish because they outsmarted him, he studied them in great detail.

Browns are the hardiest of trout because they can live in water that would kill most other fish—especially cutthroat or brook trout. Browns have been known to feed in waters with temperatures in excess of 80 degrees (85 to 86 degrees starts to become lethal). Of all the species of trout, they can live in the warmest water. In such water, most trout species would have a difficult time breathing, let alone feeding, because the oxygen they desperately need is not held effectively in the water. Browns are the most tolerant. Their optimum temperature is 55 to 65 degrees. If the water drops below 45 degrees, their body processes slow down, so they do little feeding and fishing is futile. If the water gets too warm, the fish slow down and fishing is also tough. Water warmer than the low 80s makes for hard fishing because fish likely won't bite.

As the name implies, this fish is chocolate brown as a rule, but the color varies depending on the time of year and the water conditions. Its belly is a light brown to a dull yellow. Browns also have a lovely square tail. This fish is very aggressive in its behavior, but cautious at the same time. If there was ever a time to crawl toward a pool on your hands and knees, it's when you're after a trophy brown. One slight mistake and your presence will be detected. Even the small fish will shut down if they're slightly spooked.

Browns usually aren't impressed by the flashy, gaudy flies that brookies and cuts love. You're more likely to be successful with an Adams, not a Coachman. If you're casting attractors for browns and you don't pick up a fish after a few passes, try another fly or move to another area. Unlike the rainbow, which is finicky but can eventually be enticed into hitting a fly through repeated presentation, a brown is usually definitive. If it wants a fly, it'll take it almost right away. It can rarely be teased into a strike—except during the spawn, when all rules are cast aside.

Browns are interested in realistic fly patterns. You will be more successful if you can match the actual food they are eating that day. These fish also like large insect hatches (such as stone flies), and streamers imitating fry, mice, snakes, and baby ducks. Fishing large presentations at night is an excellent way to hook big brown trout.

The best time to fish for trophy browns is during the spawn, when the fish are less wary, more protective of their waters, and are willing to strike aggressively at any intrusion. Depending on the climate, a brown spawns sometime during the fall—frequently in October or November. The decreasing temperature, shorter days, higher waters, and natural biology bring on the spawning urge (and a flock of eager anglers). Like most trout, browns spawn on the gravel bottoms in shallow water. The female scoops out some of the gravel and sand, and deposits her eggs while the male waits downstream and guards the nest. This nest is called a *redd*. When the eggs are laid, the male fertilizes them. During the spawn, the bigger males grow a wonderfully hooked jaw called a *kype*. The big fish are protective, and they'll slam into anything that comes along and bothers them. When you're fishing, look for gravel beds with cover on the sides in one to two feet of water. Also look for the dull flashes of spawning females on the redds. Brown trout should be there.

During the spawn, I usually fish a #12 Glow Bug. I've had mornings in which I caught 35 fish, never changing the pattern. My next choice for spawners is a bushy streamer—Muddler Minnow, Bucktail Streamers, or leech patterns (#4-8). Anything that looks threatening might elicit a response. The trick is to drag the fly right past the fish's nose. I use a small shot (size depends on the current), placed about six inches above my Glow Bug. I attach a strike indicator three to five feet up the leader, adjusted to the water depth. I lob my fly a few yards above the redd and let it drift naturally. The Glow Bug and the strike indicator should float with the current. When the fly gets in front of a brown, the strike will be brisk and short. You have to set the hook quickly. The spawning fish will take your fly out of anger, aggression, hunger, or conditioned response. All trout, especially browns, act this way during the spawn and are easily hooked.

Browns can grow pretty large. I've heard of a Bavarian strain that easily pushed into the high 40-pound range. The White River in Arkansas, as I mentioned, has been the home of fish growing 30 to 40 pounds. My home state of Utah boasts a number of browns taken from Flaming Gorge in the upper 30-pound range, and our Green River is a world-class fishery. Besides the well-known Madison River in southwestern Montana, there are many other blue-ribbon brown streams in North America.

This wonderful brown trout was caught during the fall spawn. Notice the "kyped" jaw.

This rainbow was caught on a Leech pattern during the spring spawn. It took nearly fifteen minutes to land.

Argentina and New Zealand also have a number of fine fishing waters.

It's best to fish for browns at dawn, at dusk, and at night. Some experts feel that night is the optimum time, because it's harder for the fish to see the angler or inspect the fly closely. Browns can be found anywhere in the stream, but as a rule they prefer slow water and pools. They aren't prolific leapers like rainbows, but they put up a wonderful, powerful fight.

Some famous brown flies to keep in your box might include: Adams, Quill Gordon, March Brown, and Light/Dark Cahill (dry); Marabou Leech, Muddler Minnow, and Bucktails (wet).

Rainbow Trout. The rainbow trout is smart, but not like a brown. This fighting fish is found in all but one or two states, in Canada (except for the Northwest Territories), and in Mexico. Rainbows grow best in 56- to 63-degree waters, but they can handle temperatures on either side of the optimum—even water into the higher 70s. I'm told there are now some hardy strains of desert rainbow that will survive in low 80-degree water like the brown, but rainbows are typically more oxygen-sensitive. Most trout can adjust to gradual temperature change like the natural change in seasonal temperatures. If the change is sudden and the fish haven't acclimatized, problems arise.

There are over 30 species of rainbow trout, plus a few variations. This hardy fish gets around and adjusts easily. It's the fish most often used in hatcheries, because it's so adaptable. If there are cutthroats in a water, it's not unusual to see some crossbreeding, resulting in cut-bows. The West is probably a better rainbow fishery overall than the East, because the water is a little faster and cleaner. Rainbows are fond of fast-moving water. When one thinks of 'bows, one thinks of running water.

Rainbows grow big like German browns. One fish caught in western Canada tipped the scales at 52 pounds. An angler can't help but observe in outdoor magazines the number of 'bows caught in the 15- through 30-pound range. Fish in rivers and streams are usually smaller than lake rainbow, but you'd be hard-pressed to keep track of the many rivers and streams that host ten-pound-plus fish.

Rainbows will eat almost anything. A brown will go for a worm or a hopper once in a while, maybe even some cheese-floating stuff, a marshmallow paste, or Power Bait. But for every brown that takes such garbage, there are several dozen rainbows eager to rush in and gulp it up.

This fish is known as a leaper. When you hook into a rainbow, it will often jump out of the water several times, trying to shake the hook. You need to keep a crisp line. This trout is also more likely to pick up a flashy fly. 'Bows aren't as easily spooked as browns are. It's often a good strategy to keep working a rainbow again and again, especially if it's feeding. A continual presentation might spook a brown, or at least fail to provoke a response. You can often tease a rainbow into striking. Maybe it decides it's hungry, or maybe it just gets mad and goes for your fly. I've caught lots of nice rainbows by casting continually.

Rainbows spawn sometime in the spring, depending on where the water is located and the water conditions. When the water gets about 55 degrees, the hen scoops out a redd in the gravel bed by lying on her side and fan-

This fine rainbow was caught on a black Woolly Worm. It was quickly released.

Jon-Michael, the author's son, gets an early start on his fishing career.

ning with her tail. She deposits her eggs, then the male fertilizes them. She goes upstream a little way and does it again. The dirt and gravel she kicks up help cover the previous redd. The process is repeated until she is spawned out. At this time, rainbows become quite colorful. Their beautiful, red rose to light scarlet streak becomes more predominant. Males get a hooked jaw and tear into each other if territorial boundaries are violated. During the spawn, a Glow Bug is again my first choice. I'm also fond of streamers and leeches. The spring spawn is considered the best time to hook a trophy. A Glow Bug that sort of simulates a fish egg can be used on rainbows year-round. In fact, rainbows are pushovers for many egg patterns.

Brook Trout. The brook trout is the dandy of trout. We adore the brown for its clever skill and coyness; we love the 'bow for its ever-presence, its cleverness, and its leaping ability. But we love the brookie for its wondrous good looks. The brook is a beautiful fish, partly because of its vermiculations. These are the dusky, wavy, wormlike lines on its very dark olive green back (the sure way to identify a brookie). Its belly is ivory, but might change to a dull red as the fish gets older. The fins often display an orange tint on larger fish. The brookie has lovely red spots inside a hazy blue border. It likes water between 57 and 61 degrees. In fact, brookies aren't found in any water that reaches a temperature beyond 68 or 69 degrees for a prolonged period of time.

To be absolutely correct, a brook trout really isn't a trout. Technically, the brookie is a char—as is the lake trout. Brookies don't grow as large as other trout. A five-pounder is an extraordinary catch. A brookie that gets to ten pounds is a monster. The world's record is 14½ pounds. Brookies are delicate. They can't take pollution or warm water. They are a high mountain or headwater fish. Traditionally an East Coast trout, they've done well in the Rocky Mountain area and in some locations on the West Coast.

I mentioned that the cutthroat is the dumbest trout. It is, but the brookie isn't any rocket scientist, either. In waters where there is very little fishing pressure, it doesn't take much more than a bare hook to fool this little jewel. In fact, on a few backcountry packing trips, I might have starved to death if it weren't for brook trout. Brookies like to hang around undercut banks and in the shade of willow trees. They like slow water, but it has to be cold and pure. The brookie is a pushover for flashy flies. A Coachman or Wulff is a good attractor to start with. The Woolly Bugger and Goofus Bug are good choices, too. Flashy streamers (with soft marabou feathers) and leech patterns are musts in your brook trout fly box. When in doubt, go with something that has red or yellow in it.

In addition to the flies we've talked about, you might want to add these to your brookie box: Black Gnats, Yellow Hackles, Black Moose. For wets, especially for big fish, go with streamers like Mickey Finns, Marabou Leech patterns, and Woolly Worms. Fish with extremes. If a dark pattern isn't working, go to a light one.

Cutthroat Trout. Maybe cutthroat trout are the dumbest, but in many ways they're my favorite. I cut my teeth on cutthroats, and they have always held a special place in my heart. When I was in the third grade, I spent a summer in the mountains near Star Valley, Wyoming, catching cutthroat after cutthroat. This is where I first learned to tell a fish tale. My son Jon-Michael caught his first fish, a two-pound cutthroat, from Yellowstone Lake two summers ago. I like to catch cuts because they're cooperative. After a day of trying to fool browns, it's nice to know that cutthroats exist.

They get big, too. The largest official specimen was taken from Nevada's Pyramid Lake, and it pushed the scale at over 41 pounds. Some anglers claim they've landed cuts over 50 pounds, but those catches are not official. In my home state of Utah, Bear Lake has produced a cut weighing almost 20 pounds and, as I mentioned earlier, Strawberry Lake boasted a 26-pounder. Obviously, big lake cuts are challenging, but they're very catchable on a fly rod. Unlike lake trout, which are deep water fish, cuts are suspended. With a sinking line and a Woolly Bugger or a leech (and patience), big fish can be yours. Nevertheless, streams and rivers are where cutthroat come into their own, and these are the waters that most fly casters focus on.

My three favorite cutthroat waters are in Yellowstone Park. The famous Yellowstone River and Yellowstone Lake are without parallel. So is Slough Creek, in the northeastern section of the park. These waters offer exciting cutthroat action that's sure to make your day. Early in the season, Yellowstone Lake can be very good casting from the bank. Later, a float tube is a must so you can get farther out. I've caught so many nice fish on this lake that I don't need to lie about how well I've done. I've had a few off days, but overall I can't praise cut fishing in the park enough. My fourth-favorite water is the Bear River on the north slope of the Uinta Mountains (south of Evanston, a few miles north of the Utah border). I've spent many fine days on the Bear, catching tons of fish in the one- to two-pound range and a few that went almost four pounds. Since the river (which is really a creek) runs through private land, it's rarely fished, and the trout are able and willing to take most of the flies you throw at them.

In streams and rivers, I've had great luck with specific imitators and with #12-16 attractors like the Adams, Yellow Hackle, Humpy, Wulff, and Coachman. I've also been successful fishing wet flies: Scuds, Hare's Ears, and Pheasant Tails, in #12-18.

As a rule, cuts aren't very wary. However, every now and then when you're fishing the high mountain lakes, you'll run into a school of fish that have gotten their Ph.D.s in avoid-ing flies. Such fish are very selective feeders. They focus on one or two common food sources, and since they don't get much variety, they avoid what they don't know. If you don't present a familiar pattern that they're used to eating, in the exact size, you aren't going to catch a fish. Period. All you'll get is casting practice.

There are 14 or 15 recognized cutthroat subspecies, in addition to a few hybrid fish. As the name implies, all cuts have one thing in common—some sort of an orange to scarlet slash under the jaw on the throat. Depending on the water, sex, and subspecies, the "cut" on the throat may be dark or light, a band or blotchy spots. You'll notice that the jaws and head of a cutthroat are a little bigger when you hold one next to its second cousin, the rainbow. The front part of the body tends to be a little thicker, too, and the cut has more colorful, larger spots. Male cuts are usually more colorful than females. Cuts that eat a steady diet of crustaceans also tend to be more brightly colored.

This fish spawns in the spring—from February to late May or early June, depending on the altitude and climate. When the water gets near 50 degrees, cuts start thinking about spawning. Even for lake cutthroat, streams are the preferred spawning area. Spawners look for gravel beds where there is a comfortable amount of oxygen in the water. The female scoops the redd out of the gravel and deposits her eggs. Then she moves upstream and repeats the process. The males fertilize eggs and fight each other while the female deposits more eggs. These fish grow and feed best in 51- to 64-degree water.

The cutthroat trout was the kingpin fish of the Rocky Mountain West until around the 1880s, when other species were introduced. With few exceptions, almost all of our famous Western brown and 'bow waters were formerly cutthroat waters. Cut territory extended from the eastern edge of the Cascades to the eastern slope of Rockies, and from southern Canada to northern Mexico. But things have changed.

Where browns, rainbows, and cuts existed in the same stream and fishing pressure was applied, cutthroats got thinned in a hurry. Browns are more wary. They adapted to fishing pressure, but the cutthroat got wiped out and other, more dominant trout filled the niche. At one time, if history isn't lying, the average fish caught during the spawn on California's Truckee River weighed 20 pounds! Not far away, on Lake Tahoe, there were so many fish that they were caught commercially and sold in the Bay Area for 40 to 50 cents a pound. That was just 50 years ago! Today, native populations have all but gone the way of the buffalo and the passenger pigeon. Only stocking keeps things going.

Cuts can be trashed easily. Do your part to ensure that they don't get fished out. Conservation now will mean cutthroats into the next century.

FISH WISH

Notes on Fishing the Spawn

The urge to mate can be the downfall of nearly all creatures—from elk to human to trout. Even the cagiest lunker waxes less-than-cautious during the spawn and becomes catchable. A river that's tough to fish any other time of the year will make you feel like a casting pro if you throw flies during the spawn. You can catch lots of fish if you're fishing around a redd.

Be careful, though. Don't kill what you love. Watch where you're walking as you wade. Don't tromp gravel areas where eggs are laid. One wrong step could kill thousands of eggs. And spawning fish are fragile. Play them quickly. Release them quickly. The further they are into the spawn, the weaker the fish will be. Respirate your fish if necessary. Keep the population healthy. It would be foolish to kill a fish at this time, preventing it from propagating. Also, spawning trout don't taste good.

I've mentioned that Glow Bugs are an excellent fly. They're my favorite for all the spawns. A Glow Bug is a clump of bright yarn tied on a hook and trimmed to look like a big salmon egg. It drives spawning trout nuts. When it passes over a spawning bed, fish hit it with a vengeance if they don't have to move too far to do it. Other species of trout, which aren't spawning but are waiting below the spawning beds for eggs that wash down off the redds, will hit this fly, too. In fact, some of the largest rainbow trout I've hooked have been caught with Glow Bugs during the brown trout spawn.

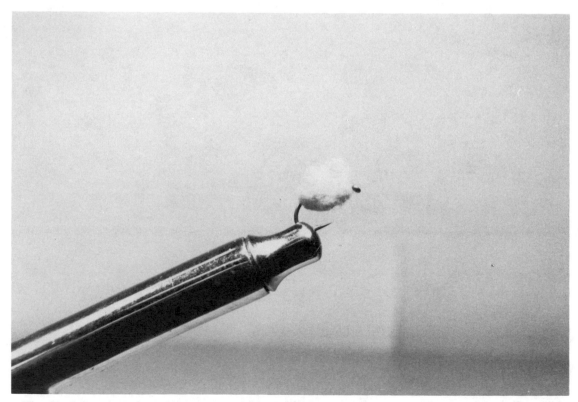

The Glow Bug is one of the most deadly wet patterns you can own. They're also easy to tie.

While this book isn't about fly tying, you can easily tie your own Glow Bugs, and it will save you a few bucks. Start with a Dai-Riki #12, 135 hook (a scud hook). There are other hook manufacturers, and many are cheaper, but Dai-Riki hooks are the sharpest and strongest. Next, "spin" on the yarn like you would the deer head hair of a Muddler Minnow. Consult any fly tying book for specific instructions on how to tie a Glow Bug. You'll save a lot of money, and it will be a good introduction to tying. In half an hour, you can tie a dozen Glow Bugs.

The spawn seems to occur during the cool or downright *cold* part of the year. While it may be spring on the calendar, so you know the 'bows are spawning, it may feel like winter is still here. The same is true of the brown spawn in the fall. As I write these lines, I've just returned from the Provo River, where it was 19 bone-chilling degrees. I caught 25 fish in half a day, and three of my toes were nearly frozen off. Sheets of ice a quarter-inch thick were frozen on my waders, and I had to clear the eyes of my rod every couple of casts. It was great fishing, but chilly.

Be prepared for the weather when you fish. I put hand warmers in each pocket, and I'm bundled so thick that I can hardly move. Over the years, I've found several things that help me beat the cold. I carry a net so I can scoop the fish up from the stream, thus keeping my hands or gloves dry. I wear something on my head. And I carry a large thermos full of black Postum. About every 15 minutes, I pour one or two ounces into the cap and drink it. A bit of warm liquid to the body core really recharges the fishing soul.

I may look stupid, but I can stay on the water a lot longer. I've got my fly in the water more often than the next guy, who has almost frozen to death. Plus, I can actually feel the rod to set the hook, unlike the angler with the iced-over hands.

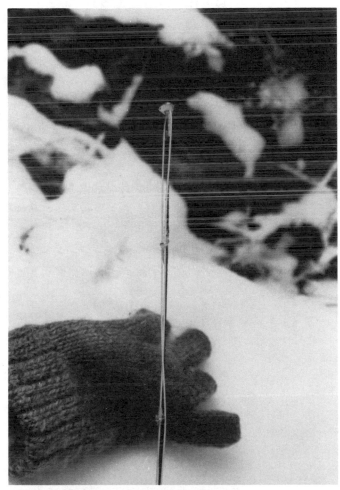

When fishing in cold weather, it's often necessary to clear ice from the eyes of the rod. Wool fingerless gloves keep your hands warm while leaving your fingers free.

Sometimes the best way to get into good salmon or steelhead country is to load up a backpack and take a hike.

TWELVE

Steelhead, Salmon, and Grayling
Some of My Favorite Friends

MY FISHING BUDDY GARY ASKED ME WHY I'D GROUP SALMON AND STEELHEAD WITH GRAYLING. "There is no logical reason," I proclaimed. "Don't try to find one."

I probably love steelhead the most. I love 'em as much as breathing hits of fresh, cold air in the Wind River Mountains of western Wyoming. But I love salmon as much as an autumn morning in the Tetons, when the elk bugle. And I love grayling the way I love a pure alpine valley with a hint of mist and grizzly tracks by the brook. These fish are some of my best friends.

The Gear

Grayling. With grayling, the lighter the rod the better. Perhaps a #4 is best. But you don't need any special equipment. Grayling aren't fussy.

Steelhead and Salmon. The clever angler might say, "Hey! There are a lot of differences between these two fish." True, but unless you're fishing for Alaskan kings, the differences are fairly subtle. For both fish, the kind of water you'll be fishing, your fishing method, the

weight of the fish, and the kind of gear you'll use will be similar.

You'll need the right kind of gear. On the Roque River last spring, I was fishing with a master river guide. We watched a grown man cry. I'd have cried, too. This fellow goofed and brought the wrong rod. It must have been a #5, but he fished anyway. He cleverly worked a nice pocket of water for quite a while. Then he got a strike. He'd hooked a really nice fish.

Because he had a light outfit, it was hard if not impossible to turn his fish in the swift current. Then the steelhead got into heavy water and really started to strip out line. The caster had some backing, but not enough. He raced down the bank to get some line back, but the mighty fish only peeled off his line faster and faster.

To add insult to injury, his backing wasn't tied very well, and it tragically snapped off the reel with a twang. This was the best steelhead he'd hooked in four years, he told us with a sob. He'd lost his $50 fly line and suffered the agony of defeat. It probably wouldn't have happened if he had brought a heavier rod and a reel with more line capacity. The man in question set his rod down and buried his head in his hands.

The Rod. Unless I'm after big Alaskan kings, my steelhead and salmon rod are the same unit. You'll need a #8 rod or larger. Your rod should be at least a nine-footer; I'm fond of 9½- or 10-foot rods. With this equipment you can cast farther, control your cast, keep your back casts off the willows, and mend your line more effectively. A fighting butt, a several-inch-long extension to the handle that can be braced against your body for extra leverage, is nice. But I can rarely find mine when I need it. For big salmon I may keep it on full-time, since it won't do me any good sitting in the storage case in my Bronco.

The Reel. You can't have too much backing on a reel used for heavy, fighting fish. You'll need a minimum of 100 yards of backing. Better yet, have 200 yards. My reel weighs only 8.5 ounces, but it holds 340 yards of 20-pound backing. When a fish strips out 100 yards of backing in one run, it's reassuring to look down and see that you have a lot more line. Salmon and steelhead are river fish, so keep in mind that a 10- or 15-pound fish can fight like a demon and strip off line like a 30-pound lake fish when current is involved. You'll also want a couple of extra spools, so you can fish effectively in the various conditions you'll encounter.

Lines. You'll need at least two lines—a floating line and some sort of wet or sinking line (which is why you'll need a couple of spools). During the average casting day, you might shift back and forth several times, depending on the water and conditions.

I've tried a number of floating lines, but a weight forward is my line of choice. You'll have to do plenty of long casting, often into gusting wind. A weight forward line gives you an edge when you're casting in wind. I'm fond of Ultra-2 Floating Line-Steelhead. It's a line designed for steelheaders and salmon folks by people who actually fish. It's a line that shoots well, too. Some steelhead line tapers too rapidly into the fine running line, which makes mending problematic. Ultra-2 or a specialized line like it has a different core and a long belly and taper. It's a cinch to mend and easy to roll cast. In the old days, you used whatever line you could get. Nowadays, specialized lines are designed for more specific types of fishing. They can make an average angler more successful with less effort.

For wet fly fishing, I usually use a sinking tip instead of an "official" wet line. I may couple this with a weighted fly or lead on the line. Of late, because I like the dry line so well, I've become converted to the Ultra-2 Wet Tip Steel Head Taper. This line lets me get my fly down, and I have good control.

Steelhead

I was hooked on steelhead before I picked up a rod. As I mentioned earlier, I used to sit in my sixth-grade class and watch the steelhead casters on the Rogue River. I vowed that I'd be one someday, too. I was too young to know that it was a cult, but I would gladly have joined the movement at age 11.

To misquote Robert Browning (or maybe to say what he really meant), "When the steelhead are running, all is right with the world." If you're a *cult* steelheader—whether you use a spinning rod or a fly rod—you'll know what this means. Simply the word *steelhead* is enough. Steelheading is more of a religion than a passion—although it's a passion, too. Deliberating on this member of the trout family is enough to get any fervent worshipper up in the freezing predawn, happy at the prospect of wading into bitter-cold water day in and day out. There's nothing quite like the silver flash of a steelhead when it plows out of the water and performs acrobatics in midleap.

The Fish Itself. Steelhead are seagoing rainbow trout. They get big. The record fly line fish is in the 30-pound range, and the biggest free line fish is in the 40-pound range. Unconfirmed but reputable sources say that a few fish might even make it into the 50s. Still, on a fly rod, a five-pounder lifts your spirits. A 10-pounder makes you feel like you're something special. A 15-pounder makes you feel like you're God's gift to the angling world, and a 20-pounder makes you proud to be one of the chosen few in the universe.

Steelhead can spawn several times, whereas salmon die after spawning once. Depending on its genetic coding, a steelhead will spawn at different times of the year. A winter fish will make its way up the water for the winter run; a fall or summer fish will make its way up during the fall or summer. Many steelhead runs, including those on the Rogue, are fairly well delineated.

When a seagoing steelhead hits fresh water, it's Old Home Week. Without thinking, it knows exactly where to go. Buck steelhead are usually the first to arrive upriver, making the place nice and cozy for the hens that come later. The same spawning beds are used year after year. The female lays eggs on the gravel bed, a plate-sized hollow scooped about eight inches deep by tail-fanning. The water is from one to five feet deep, with good oxygenation. Males fight each other for the right to fertilize the eggs. The hen lays her eggs, then goes upstream a way, scoops another indentation, and spawns again.

With luck, a steelhead fry will battle its way out of the gravel spawning beds, survive, swim to the ocean, and grow up. One to four years later, if it survives in the ocean, it will make its way back up the river to spawn in its birthplace. In the meantime, the adult steelhead that survive the ordeal of propagating will rest a bit before drifting back to the ocean, where they feed and regain all the energy they've lost by trying to reproduce. If they're lucky, they will return and spawn again. Some fish lose 35 to 40 percent of their body weight during this process. As a rule, the males get battered up pretty badly.

How to Fish for Steelhead. A first-timer can do it himself and be successful, but if you can swing a guide for the first day or so, you'll be light-years ahead of the game.

Do steelhead eat when they spawn? No. But this is actually an advantage, because you don't have to worry about matching the hatch. As a fish begins its journey, certain physiologi-

Steelhead fishing is a cult, a passion, and a religion. This nice steelhead was taken on a Black/Olive Weighted Leech in southern Oregon.

cal changes start to take place—the desire to eat is one of the first things to go. As it gets closer to its final destination, a fish lives off its stores of bodily fat. The feeding urge has shut down, but steelhead still act out feeding responses. While they don't eat *per se,* they take certain flies that drift right by their mouths out of reflex or habit. For some reason, salmon eggs and small insects still look appealing to the large, seagoing rainbow—even though these are a far cry from the tasty squid and fish that steelhead devour in the ocean. Some experts feel that spawning steelhead are resorting to early, pre-ocean feeding responses when they go for a fly. Maybe the fish think and feed like they did when they were young river fish. Perhaps the fly is an annoyance, or the fish are acting out aggressive behavior. For those of us who like to catch fish, it's a good thing steelhead act this way. Otherwise, they'd be tough to catch without a stick of dynamite or a big gill net.

What fly casters try to do is come up with the fly pattern and color that will trigger a response. We don't care if the fish is motivated by anger, aggression, annoyance, or an old feeding pattern, just as long as the steelie strikes our fly when we cast it.

Know When They Run. It's useless to fish in a river if the steelhead or salmon aren't there. The first thing you have to do is find out whether the fish are running. You need up-to-date information. You can get at least a general idea by looking in books and magazines. In many areas, the runs are predictable. Be a detective. Call guides, tackle stores, bait shops, sporting goods stores, and the local game and fish office for the hottest information.

Know Where to Fish. There's a lot of river, and most of it won't have steelhead in it. You have to focus on the right water. You need to look for the migrating paths the steelhead take up the river and places where the steelhead rest. You can catch fish in the migratory paths, but you're better off focusing your efforts on resting places.

When you look at the water, look for the easiest access up the stream. The migrating fish will take the course of least resistance to conserve their energy. We may not notice them, but there are watery "roads" that spawning fish travel. Every so often, as you'd expect, the fish needs to rest or hold. Fish rest in the water that taxes them least, and this is where you want to fish. A group of steelhead might hold over for a day, a few hours, or just a few minutes. Remember that a good resting water remains a good resting water. If it holds one group of fish now, it will hold others later.

Many resting waters are known, and anglers sometimes race to stake out a claim on a favorite spot. The caster who gets there first gets the best fishing. Many good holding waters are charted, and are a matter of record. A little research will give you a good idea where you might like to start. You can find detailed information in books that describe the specific water you plan to fish or from local anglers.

Use common sense. If you were a weary fish swimming up current, how would you get through the fast stuff? Where does the water look calm enough to lie in? After a long riffle or a series of rougher waters, a calm pool is a likely holding area. For fly casting, water that's two to seven feet deep is optimum. Depending on the water you're fishing in, you'll use a three- to thirteen-foot leader. The short leaders are for sinking lines, and the long leaders are for dry lines. I wouldn't use less than an eight-pound test leader.

For more information, Scientific Anglers has produced two excellent videos on steelhead that you might look into. They are as helpful as anything I've seen, and they're worth serious study for the earnest steelheader. My favorite, *Fishing for Pacific Steelhead*, was shot near my old stomping grounds in Oregon.

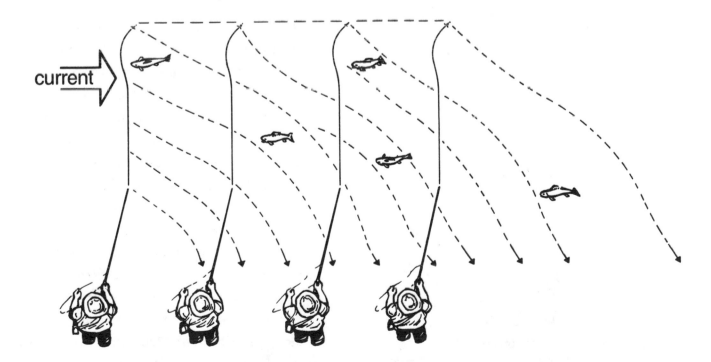

To get more depth from your swing, cast across the current and let the fly sink with the current.

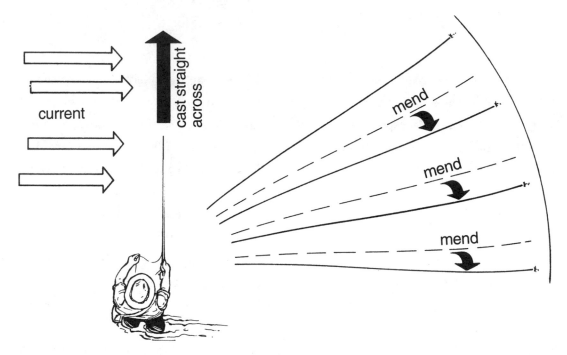

The downward swing. This cast will help you cover the water and allow you to present your fly to any fish that are in the area. Cast out and let your line swing downstream. Cast out again, but this time a foot closer. Continue until your line is right in front of you. If you get no response, move a step or two downstream, and continue casting there.

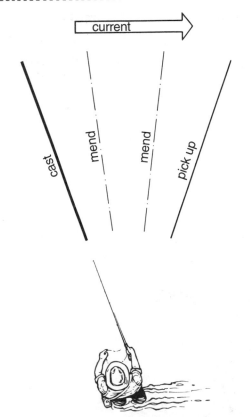

The quartering cast for steelhead fishing. Again consider yourself casting against a large clock, only now the clock is horizontal. With the upstream direction as 12:00, cast to 2:00. Let the fly drift straight down, mending as needed. At 4:00, pick up and cast again.

Fishing Strategies. It's often hard to feel the pickup, because steelhead are light biters. Don't get anxious. Wait until you feel the pull before you set the hook. Make sure you sharpen your hooks, since you'll have to work hard to get a single strike. It would be a shame to miss a fish because of a dull hook.

When you fish, you need to work the water. Use a systematic method for covering the patch of river you've selected. There are a number of traditional casting methods you might employ. But there are two that cover many of the fishing situations you will encounter: the *down-swing* and the *short down-swing* (a shortened version of the down-swing) casts. Both casts allow you to work systematically, so your fly covers a lot of water effectively. Catching steelhead isn't luck. It's carefully calculated work, and it's a lot of fun.

Salmon are a challenge and a thrill with a fly rod. King salmon like this one test both the caster and the equipment. I caught this Alaskan king about 75 miles northwest of Anchorage. Notice the kyped, or hooked, jaw.

Salmon

Is there anything as tempting as catching salmon with a fly rod? Not if you live in the Pacific Northwest, near the Great Lakes, or on the Atlantic seaboard. Jack salmon, chinook salmon, king salmon, Atlantic salmon, Alaskan king salmon, dog salmon, pink salmon, red salmon, coho salmon, chum salmon—by any name, salmon is king. Nothing tops the splendidly electrical charge a fighting salmon gives you when you catch it on a fly.

When I was 12, I caught my first chinook with my father off the Brookings coast in southern Oregon. Even though I was using shark tackle, it was fun. Several years later, I landed my first midsize salmon on a fly rod, and I've never been the same. My mother says that's when I started going off the deep end. I looked down and saw how lovely that big fish was, and I thought about how damn clever I was for hooking it. I went all warm and fuzzy.

Fishing for Salmon. As with steelhead, read the water. Many steelhead fishing techniques are also used when you're casting for salmon. You have to find out where they hold. Look for migration routes through the least-taxing water. What's the easiest way to get up a riffle or a set of rapids? Where would the fish rest after making such an ascent? You'll catch fish when you fish where they hold.

Once I've found the right water, I like to drift my fly slowly across the fish's nose. Spawning salmon don't eat, but they hit flies out of reflex or aggression. The bite is often very slight. It's important to keep a tight line, so you can set the hook (which must be sharp). A salmon won't go very far out of its way to take a fly. You have to get it right to the fish. That's why it's so important to cover the water thoroughly.

I like to start with flashy colors. However, I have flies that cover the complete spectrum. Equally important, I like to have flies with full bodies as well as flies that are sparsely tied. There are times when a bulky fly seems to do

the trick. At other times, fish hit more steadily on sparse flies. I can find no rhyme or reason for it. You have to experiment until you get the right combination. I tie some patterns weighted with about six twists of lead, and some without weight. Sometimes you'll fish the fly dry. At other times, you'll use weight on the line or a weighted pattern. It depends on the water. I like to be armed for every situation.

Grayling

Going after grayling is a quest for purity. It's not just *catching* grayling that makes you feel good. They aren't difficult to hook. It's more. To quote Brother Walton, a grayling is

Grayling are delicate fish, and you should be very careful when releasing them. Don't play them longer than you have to, and return them to the water quickly. Notice the prominent dorsal fin.

"simpler than a trout; for he will rise twenty times at a fly—if you miss him—and yet rise again."

It's not just the wonderful hues of purple, or the dorsal fin with the fluorescent sapphire dots, or the grayling's cute white lips. At first, a grayling fights like a bulldog. When it realizes that the struggle is useless, it gives up. If a grayling reaches two pounds, it's quite the trophy.

It's not just the long-range grayling eye, which lets the fish spot a struggling mayfly on the film 13 watery feet away, shoot after it, and, at the moment of truth, myopically miss its prey and have to attack again. There's more to it.

I religiously quest after *Thymallus arcticus* several times a year. I'm not sure if it's a quest for the fish, which is wholly pure, or for the world that the fish lives in, which is also wholly pure. Since the grayling is innocent, it's rightly known as gullible and easy to catch. It has never evolved the caginess or suspicion of the brown, the guile of the walleye, or the tenacity of the rainbow.

You have to admire a fish that survives without learning to distrust the universe from which it has evolved. Doubt never enters its simple mind. The grayling isn't aware that there is evil out there until it's too late, and even then one wonders if its innate gullibility is ever challenged. It can live only in the cleanest, gin-clear water. If something looks like food, the grayling assumes that it must be food. Artificiality is never considered, so this fish will take almost any fly that looks somewhat real. For that matter, it will take anything that looks like an insect. The grayling should be our environmental barometer.

Grayling fishing is an at-oneness. The species reminds the fly caster of what the earth was like before things started to sneak up on other things—before Watergate, before computers, before deception. Its Eden-like innocence is most refreshing in the midst of our twentieth-century madness.

The grayling is gullible, but it's a tough little cold-water fish. In many of the streams or lakes it inhabits, ice is a major factor. In fact, in some parts of the grayling's world, ice is a reality eight to ten months a year. As you might suspect, the water in many of these regions is oxygen-depleted, so trout wouldn't thrive. The grayling fits the niche nicely and does quite well; it even seems to flourish. It requires considerably less oxygen than trout.

Canada and Alaska have uncharted tracts of excellent grayling water. But the mountainous Western regions of the United States also contain very fishable populations of grayling. The fish that lives here is referred to as the Montana Grayling. High alpine lakes and streams—especially those that can't host trout—make good homes for grayling. Montana probably has the most grayling waters. Lately, however, some of the largest fish have been caught in Wyoming. Last summer, I was lucky enough to catch several fish at the top of the grayling trophy scale—fish that weighed two pounds.

There are grayling in many Western states—most notably in Montana, Wyoming, Colorado, Idaho, and Washington. Even the lower mountains states like Utah have many good grayling waters. When you head into the backcountry, check the local angling guidebook.

How to Catch Grayling. One of the great joys of grayling fishing is taking them on a dry fly. If there's any sort of a hatch going on, you'll probably encounter grayling action. It's nice if you can match the hatch, which will almost instantly ensure fish. But almost any pattern of caddis or mayfly will be successful. Several attractor patterns seem to work no matter what the fish are actually hitting. Among these are the Gray Hackle Yellow, Black Gnat, Adams, Royal Coachman, and Griffith's Gnat.

On rivers, I fish my flies in a dead drift with no drag. On lakes, I'll let the fly lie on the film for a while. Then, very slowly, I'll start to retrieve it. I experiment. If this doesn't work, I'll retrieve it more quickly. While this might be a little unnatural, grayling often tend to hit a moving fly.

Every now and then, there's no action on the surface. Perhaps there's not a hatch on, it's the wrong time of the day, the fish are gorged, or the light or temperature is too extreme. For whatever reason, the fish are deep. Go to Plan B, and use the wet fly.

Wet fly sizes for grayling are from #14-20. The optimum size is #16-18. On streams, I'll fish a Pheasant Tail or a Hare's Ear and let it dead drift. On lakes, you have to vary the approach. One day on my favorite lake in the Wind River Mountains, the surface water was dead. Nothing was active on the film. We decided to work it anyway. None of us could get a rise out of the infinite number of dry flies we tried. A good fishing buddy finally slipped on his wet spool, tied on a wet fly, and started casting. We were all so busy that we hadn't paid attention. Within 20 minutes, he caught and released five nice fish. We all switched over to wet or weighted lines and pulled in fish almost every cast.

Just about any wet fly works, but I've found several that produce better than most: a black or olive Woolly Bugger (or a black/olive combination); a Black, Green, or White Leech with a long tail; or a Muddler Minnow. This is one case in which a weighted fly is very handy.

I cast out as far as I can and let the line sink for a set number of counts. Then I strip the line back in a short jigging motion, letting it drop before starting again. If I don't get a response, I'll count further, letting it drop more. I want to find the bottom. As I fish, I'll vary the retrieve and try to determine which retrieve seems to attract the most fish.

If I start catching fish I'll stay put, because these fish seem to school up. If I haven't caught a fish in 15 or 20 minutes, I'll move to a new spot and start again. Using this technique, I've rarely been skunked. Even when the film is cold, there's plenty of grayling action on the bottom.

THIRTEEN

Bass

Sacred Prey of Southern Gentlemen (and Ladies)

OBVIOUSLY, SOUTHERN GENTLEMEN AREN'T THE ONLY ONES WHO PREY ON THE BASS. Rumors of good fishing drifted northward from the quiet bayous, the big dams, and the muddy rivers of the South. Hints that bass might be more than just a common trash fish began to surface.

The notion was quickly dispelled by Southerners. Nevertheless, a few decades ago, the bass was let out of the bag, so to speak. Even Western types who were raised on blue-ribbon trout, steelhead, and salmon caught the bug. Bass fever hit big—especially among the spin casting set. Later an enlightened few, hoping they wouldn't get laughed out of the water, suggested that bass were *fantastic* on a fly rod. At the time, the purist stone flier would cough politely, as if someone had suggested a "four-letter word" like Power Bait, live bait, or worms. The casting snobs turned up their dry fly noses and changed the subject to spring creeks, dry hatches, long leader, and delicate presentations. But like a voice in the wilderness, the bass fly fishers called again: "Make way for bass with a fly rod!"

The time has come for bass and fly rods. The two go together like peaches and cream, grits and gravy, or flies and leader.

Fly Rod Bass. The bass may not replace the brown, the steelhead, or the salmon in your book, but this old lunker is great sport. I've really enjoyed going after bass—or should I say sunfish? The scientific name is *Micropterus salmoides*

Bass fishing has become popular with the general angler, who has mountains of specialized rods, reels, and tackle to match every sort of bassing situation. It has also caught on with the caster, and for good reason. In shallow water, a fly caster can generally fish bass more effectively than a spinning/bait caster. Why? Because a fly caster can present a boundless selection of food imitations that a bass might eat during any given season in any given stretch of water. In many settings, the traditional spinning approach is more restrictive. The fly caster can tempt the bass with small, natural-looking tidbits, flies more in line with its aquatic menu. The only time the fly caster is at a disadvantage is when the fish are in deep water or are suspended. Otherwise, a fly rod is a great bass tool.

What to Use. A bass caster need never feel under-gunned with a trusty fly rod. However, your bass rod ought to be at least nine feet long; I like mine 9½ feet and stiff. You'll need to throw a heavier line so you can turn over a large fly. I've become fond of a #8 line (a #7-8 weight outfit is about standard). You have to consider the potentially heavy weight of the bass and the structure you'll be fishing in. Make sure you have plenty of backing, because even a midsize bass can put up quite a fight, stripping out lots of line. Depending on the water, your leader should be 4X to 1X. A heavy, stiff leader is a necessity.

Bass are wide-bodied, so they put a lot of strain on your gear. They're hard fighters that usually take your presentation with a vengeance. There's nothing delicate about this brawling sunfish. A four- or five-pound largemouth makes you feel like you've hooked into a truck. You'll be glad you have backing. When

you have a good fish on your line, you wonder if you tied those knots carefully enough, and whether they're going to hold.

In the Great Basin where I live, the month of May or the first part of June is bass time. I try to clear my calendar and focus on this Southern transplant. Since the water in Deer Creek is clear, the bass are wonderfully colored. They're dark olive green on top and lighter olive with a dark stripe on the sides, and they have an icy, dirty white or yellowish belly. In cloudy water, they have less color.

When you hook up with six pounds of fighting sunfish, you'll be hooked on bass and a fly rod. Picture this:

It's mid-May. There are maybe two or three boats on the lake, and they're at least five miles away. Few anglers are out for bass in Utah. You're sitting in your canoe with your trusty rod. There's a nip to the early morning breeze. The spring runoff has caused the water to flood around the foliage. The nose of your canoe is wedged between an old fence post and a bunch

The largemouth bass.

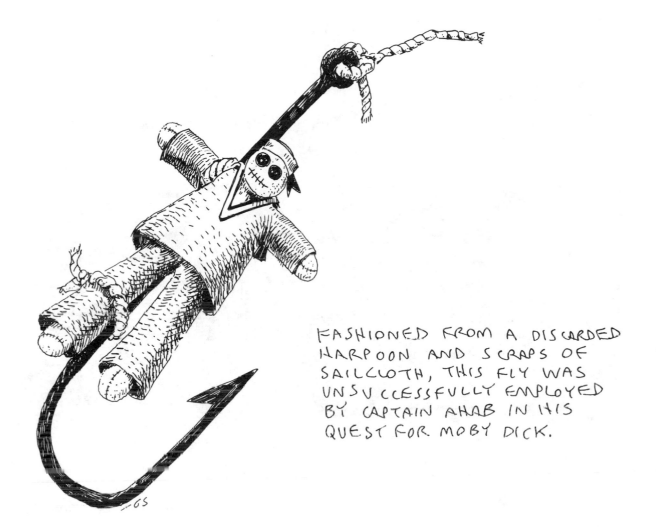

FASHIONED FROM A DISCARDED HARPOON AND SCRAPS OF SAILCLOTH, THIS FLY WAS UNSUCCESSFULLY EMPLOYED BY CAPTAIN AHAB IN HIS QUEST FOR MOBY DICK.

of brush. In front of you toward the shore is a series of willows, rushes, and fallen logs—lovely spring bass structure.

Without a second thought, you tie on a Muddler and cast toward the shadowy willows. After working the willows near a fallen log, you let the bulky fly sink and start to strip it back in short, whipping motions. After several strips . . . *WHAM!* You've hooked your first bass of the season. It's the best bass of the year, at least so far. It can only get better.

You're quite careful, because it's bad luck to lose your first largemouth of the spring. It's only a one-pounder, but you'd swear it was Moby Dick. The nine-foot rod feels great as it throbs under the fish's struggle. Eventually, you let the little lunker go.

How to Fish Bass. Here's the first rule of thumb: *Always fish in.* What is fishing in? It's fishing from deep to shallow water, from "out to sea" toward the bank. When you bass fish, you need to work the shore and structure care-

Using a canoe is an excellent way to fish for bass on a lake or pond.

fully. To fish in, you have to move around. Unless it's the only way to get there, wading is too slow, and you can't cover enough water. Besides, wading is sometimes too disruptive. A small craft like a canoe, a Porta-Bote, a float tube, or a small rowboat is perfect for shallow water. I suppose a powerful bass boat would work, too. However, I like the small, quiet equipment I can strap on my Bronco—crafts that I can carry to and from the lake or river.

Casting in offers a number of advantages. You can work a lot of water effectively. You can pull hooked fish away from shore structure or weeds that might snap your leader. You have less chance of getting hung up, because fish hold on the deep side of the structure, which is closest to you. You have better access to the deep side of the structure, where the fish are. Your movements can be masked more easily, because the fish's attention is usually directed toward shore—not in your direction. And finally, you're in a better position to read the water.

The Nature of the Largemouth. Bass come into shallow water because the temperature is more suitable, and because the shallows are a great place to feed. Bass are mighty predators, and they're called largemouth for a reason—their jaws extend beyond their eyes. "Nature gave 'em big mouths because they love to eat," my fishing buddy Gary always says. "And they don't get big by bein' stupid!"

A bass soon learns it can't get prey in the open water. It's not a fast-swimming fish, nor is it willing to chase its food for long. It's not built for distance, but rather for short, powerful, frenetic bursts and a mighty gulp. The largemouth likes to ambush its food. It hides, ambushes its prey, hides, attacks, and so on. It's an energy-efficient eating machine. Be thankful the bass isn't bigger, or you wouldn't want to dangle your legs beneath a float tube in the fish's territory.

Like the trout, the bass likes to use feeding lanes. It moves from the deep water to the shallows, or "from its bedroom to the kitchen" as Gary is fond of saying. The successful fly caster should work the fly over as many likely places as he can, trying to provoke a hiding bass into striking.

Another advantage to fishing in is that you can cover deep water, too. You'll do better fishing in the kitchen, but every now and then you'll get a hungry lunker cruising to and fro, looking for a snack—or you'll catch a hungry one in the bedroom. Remember not to overlook any stretch of water that might hold a fish. Play the percentages, and cover the water as thoroughly as you can.

The Right Bass Line. A while ago, I was bassing with a good friend. We were fishing a hot set of bass ponds near Duchesne, Utah. Both of us were using identical gear. As we worked around the cliffs, we took turns fishing the best-structured areas. After four or five hours, Alan said, "What in the name of blazes am I doing wrong? You're catching all the fish, and I've caught two."

I handed Alan my rod and told him to try it. "Same rod, same reel, same exact fly," he said. "But after this much of nothing, I'll give it a try. Am I holding my mouth wrong?"

After a while, he started getting lots of bass, while I managed to hook just two. In fact, he caught a four-pounder. For Utah, that's a pretty good fish.

What made the difference? The only difference was our choice of wet fly lines. Let's look at this line business more closely. A bass will work top water with a vengeance for a short period of time each day, or perhaps for a longer period when the water conditions are right. At times like this a good floating line is in order, and you're entitled to enjoy the devil out of it. There's nothing like a big bass on the film going after a dry pattern. However, bass like water in the mid-70s (from 74 to 76 degrees), so most of the time you won't be fishing the surface—unless you need casting practice.

Generally, it's necessary to go down deep to where the fish are, so naturally you'll be fishing with a sinking line. If you aren't careful, and if you don't use the right line, you'll be fishing with a belly (a big sag). Like Alan, you won't be catching much. The fish may be going for your offering all day, but you'll never know it. The problem is response time. The belly drag dramatically retards any indication you have of a strike, because it has to be pulled straight before you know you have an interested fish. The largemouth will pick up and spit out your fly before you have a chance to set the hook (or even before you know it's there), because you haven't felt a pickup. If you *do* feel it, it's too late.

When you fish deep for bass, feel is critical and eliminating the belly is really important. You need a direct line to the fish. I suggested to Alan that he should use a sinking line. This kind of line makes all the difference. It will allow you to present your fly most accurately.

How do you actually fly fish for bass? We've looked at some of the basic bass strategies and habits. Next, consider dividing bass fishing into three basic strategies, because you have to employ different fishing methods to be successful. Water temperatures, breeding urges, food supply, and cover have a great influence on how you'll fish. But most importantly, let's take a look at how to catch bass in each season—spring/fall fishing, spawn fishing, and summer fishing.

Spring/Fall Bass Fishing

Spring and fall fishing are similar, in that the water is cool. In the spring and fall, shallow water is the most comfortable for bass and offers the most food. The best starting place is the water near the shoreline. This is the first water to warm up after winter, and it's the last place to get cold in the fall. Here, the water temperature is more comfortable for the wily largemouth. Warm temperature is also better suited to insect life and fry, so the pickings are easier.

In the spring, bass are trying to put on the feed bag to regain the reserves they've lost over the long winter. They eat voraciously, in order to pack on extra ounces. Nevertheless, their metabolism is a little sluggish in early spring, because the water is still cold. In the fall, bass eat everything in sight. Nature has instilled a sense of urgency, so their feeding at times seems almost hysterical. Like bears, fish are storing up energy. As the water gradually cools, fish metabolism slows proportionately as a means of saving energy.

The key to finding bass in the spring and fall is fishing the shallow structured areas near

Bass and fly rods are a lot of fun.
To remove the hook, hold the fish by its lower lip.

the shoreline. At this time, they feed on as many high-energy minnows and tasty bugs as they can find. Since you know that largemouth are focusing on the shallow water near the structure and that the focus food is minnows, you're wise to start out with a minnow imitation. A streamer or a minnow pattern is my first choice. But don't overlook other proven spring/fall bass tempters: the leech, the frog, and, in the fall, the tempting hopper. While there are other routes, these standard patterns will serve you well.

I like leeches tied with a bulky body and a generous tail. I like frogs tied on the large side. A special treat for bass is a nice hopper. In the late summer and early fall, hoppers can be the most deadly pattern you throw.

Flies to Use. I've found the following flies essentials for my bass box. In fact, I carry little else when I'm bassing. I've listed them in the order of their importance for me in my part of the world. In different waters, the order could be shifted and others substituted. However, with these six patterns in a few different sizes, I feel I could catch spring/fall bass almost anywhere.

Muddler Minnow: An essential for trout and bass. This pattern is supposed to imitate a sculpin, but it's an ideal general minnow pattern, too. It works well on or near the surface or bumping the bottom. Some tie it weighted, but I like a more natural drift, so I use a sinking line or shot. To me, the weighted Muddler is clumsy. Sizes for bass: #1-8. #4-6 are my favorite sizes.

Leech: Call me sentimental. I almost always use a black or dark green/olive leech with a bulky body and a large tail for all trout types, steelhead, walleye, pike, and bass. I'm a great admirer of the leech, and I consider it to be one of the best all-around flies. This pattern represents not only a leech, but also a minnow. Sizes for bass: #2-8. #4-6 are my favorite sizes.

*A Muddler Minnow is deadly
on bass and other large predatory fish.*

*A custom leech pattern with eyes.
The eyes add weight and may make it look more lifelike.*

Frog Patterns: Frogs are killers, especially if you fish them where shallow and deep waters meet. I've never been too fussy about frogs, so long as they look froggy. Sizes for bass: #1-2.

Bucktail Streamers/King Streamers: I'm not too particular about streamers, and I'm not choosy about colors, although I'm more partial to feathers than hair. Sizes for bass: #2-12. #6 is my favorite size.

Hoppers: I use hoppers the least often, but when I do use them, they work better than any other top water fly. Get them as close as you can to the size and color of the hoppers in your area. Fish close to the shore, and watch what happens. Sizes for bass: #1-10. #4-6 are my favorite sizes.

Poppers: Poppers usually float on the surface. They make a splashing, popping sound when retrieved and attract aggressive bass. Any style. Sizes for bass: #1-5.

Now that you're armed with the right flies, the next thing to do is to fish them properly.

How to Fish Bass in Cool Water. Bass have the slows, but they're still hungry. They want it all, but they're not willing to work hard to get it. In my experience, *how* you fish for largemouth is more critical than what you fish with. When the water is cool, a fish can't expend more energy than it collects when it goes after a bite to eat. A fast retrieve that might excite bass to a frenzy in the summer, during late

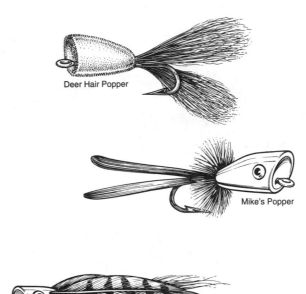

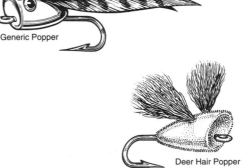

Bass flies.

spring, or in early fall will spook the same fish now—or at least it won't result in a strike. If you're thinking like a fish, you've already reached this conclusion: In cool water, use a slow retrieve.

When the water is warm, it's not unnatural for a bass to shoot off the bottom of the lake or scoot ten feet in a hurry to gulp down a tasty morsel. But in cool water, you have to drag your pattern past its nose. Your presentation needs to be thorough and deliberate. You'll probably have to let your fly sink deeper, cast close to dangerous structure (risking more hang-ups), and slow down your retrieves.

The most important thing to remember is slowing down your fly. You must work your pattern ever so lethargically. Instead of a pull, try a twitch. Instead of waiting a second or less between movements, wait two, three, or five seconds. Fish in slow motion. Use less weight, a slower sinking tip or line, or a non-weighted pattern.

After you cast, twitch your minnow, streamer, leech, or frog and let it sit. If you aren't used to this, it's hard to let your pattern just hold in the water. Wait. Now twitch it just a mite. Wait. Twitch it. Then let it sink for a few seconds. Make your pattern act like a real, if stupid, version of something tasty. If there's one mistake a bass caster commonly makes in cool water, it's moving the fly pattern too quickly.

Spawn Bass Fishing

Fishing the bass spawn usually makes you feel like you're better at this game than you really are. Of course, the same can be said for fishing during the brown, rainbow, walleye, or mackinaw spawn. A spawn makes you feel good. You're on top of the casting world.

A normal, serious fish that flits at the sight of a wispy shadow gets punch-drunk during the spawn. All good fish sense goes out the window. It's ready to take on the world, and it's afraid of nothing. Instead of displaying all the natural wariness bass are noted for, the old largemouth is in love. This is good news for

the fly caster. Just about anything you throw is liable to get gulped or attacked in anger.

Different waters warm up at different times, and the spawn is governed accordingly. When the consistent water temperature averages around 62 to 64 degrees, the bass spawn occurs.

Pre Spawn. When temperatures average in the mid-50s, bass start to move to shallow, warm water. At this time, they eat as if there was no tomorrow, trying to acquire those extra calories. When bass eat in preparation for the winter, they're also eating in preparation for mating. They eat like crazy, then prepare for the spawn by going on a semi-fast. At this time, they're very aggressive. They angrily attack nearly anything in front of them. Even sloppy casts and presentations will work. The fish are especially vulnerable to flies on the film.

Spawn. Bass must have studied feminist criticism in college. The male builds the nest, most often on sand or gravel or in mats of vegetation. He then makes a circular depression four to seven inches deep and about three feet wide. The female deposits 5,000 to 30,000 eggs, but she doesn't stick around. She heads off to the deep water, relaxing after the rigors of motherhood while the male watches over the home, keeping it tidy by fanning the water with his fins. In five to ten days, depending on water temperature, baby bass appear. Until the babies are out of the nest, the male takes on anything smaller than a Jet Ski that happens to wander too near his nest. To say he's protective is an understatement. My favorite fly at this time is a Black/Olive Leech on a #2 hook. It makes the male madder than a hornet. I like to use a wet or sink tip line and strip my Marabou Streamer a foot or so across the bottom.

After the little bass leave the nest, the male heads off to the deep water for a little R&R before going on a feeding frenzy. He may even eat his own children if they are foolish enough to get in his way.

Here are several flies I think you'll find helpful during the spawn:

Marabou Leech: Work around the areas you suspect might have nests, about a foot above the bottom. Then work through deep water to pick up post-spawn feeders. Use a black or olive pattern, #2-4.

Muddler Minnow: Work around the nesting area, where the bass will be threatened. Work in deeper water to pick up post-spawn feeders. Fish with #1-6.

Royal Coachman: Fish both wet and dry, before and after the spawn. Use #4-12.

Poppers: Almost any popper with legs, twitched over the film, is a killer if bass are taking from the surface. Use bigger sizes.

Summer Bass Fishing

When the water starts to warm up during the summer months, fishing is very good. However, it often slacks off during the heat of the day. Fish the early mornings and late evenings,

near shore and structure. Where it's legal, fishing after dark is even better—especially when it's hot. In late July and August, I like to fish from 6 p.m. until midnight. Bass still come into the shallow water to feed, but they don't stay there when dinner is over. They go back to more comfortable waters. For the record, water temperatures from 65 to 75 degrees are comfortable.

Time of Day. Many bass casters make the fatal mistake of fishing at the wrong time. Fishing early and late is the key. Late morning and afternoons are usually pretty slow. You might pick up a few odd fish at these times, but the percentages aren't in your favor unless you get really deep. When the temperature drops, your chances go up.

Bass in the Structure. Sometimes in summer, the shallow waters (where hunting is best) aren't the most suitable temperature for bass. So they come in to hunt, then head back into the deep water, where it feels more comfortable. When it gets a little cooler—in the early morning, late afternoon, and night—the water in the kitchen may not be quite optimum, but it feels better than it does in the middle of the day.

When the sun is low, try fishing the top water near the structure, meaning the shore, the weeds, and the reeds. Don't miss anything that looks likely. If there's shade on the water, fish it. Lunkers are lurking around, looking for an easy meal. The sides of a fallen log and undercut banks are likely, too. Bass are in this water to eat.

Cast beyond the target area, and work your fly across the suspected strike zone. Cast as close to the shore, the reeds, the weeds, or the snag as you can. Try to imitate the real thing. Make your fly swim like a frog, a leech, or a hopper. A frog starts and stops and rests. A leech darts erratically. A hopper struggles to get out of the water. Experiment with your fly.

Your retrieve is what gives most flies life—or at least the extra edge. Try a number of variations. At different times of the year, different moves will excite fish. Here's a rule of thumb: In cold water, move slowly; in warm water, move fast. Sometimes a splash and a struggle is just what the doctor ordered. The only exception is the frog, which always seems to work best when it's retrieved slowly.

**This white bass was taken on a White Marabou Leech.
Panfish grow so fast that it's often okay to take stringer home.**

This lake trout was taken on a Black Leech on the Wyoming side of Flaming Gorge.

FOURTEEN

Lake Trout and Whitefish

Worth Considering

YOU MIGHT THINK A LAKE TROUT OR MACKINAW IS A DEEP WATER FISH. IT IS. You might think that since it's a deep water fish, it's not likely prey for the fly caster. Not so.

While the mackinaw isn't perfectly made to order for the fly outfit, it can provide you with excellent sport. If you live near mack waters, you ought to look into dropping a fly for this deep water predator. The first time you get a lake trout snatching up your wet fly, whether it be a jig, a Woolly Bugger, or a Muddler Minnow, you'll wonder why you didn't go for this veritable Jaws sooner. You'll think you've latched onto a freight train. The word *fight* will take on a new, special meaning. A good-sized fish can take over an hour to land!

Getting the Fly Down. How do you get your fly down to deep water fish? Good question. Mackinaw are known for holding in 75 to 100 feet of water. When they are this deep, there's not much you can do. While a good solid bass rod and a heavy jig might do the trick, this kind of depth is something a fly rod isn't designed for. So how do you catch one of these monsters on the sublime piece of gear known as a fly rod?

You have to learn something about lake trout. Knowledge is power. I'm not the world's greatest lake trout fisherman, but I know enough about the species to catch them regularly. There are three things you have to keep in mind: feeding habits, water temperature, and the spawn. If you just go out and throw a line, you might catch fish, but you probably won't catch a mack.

Feeding Habits. These lunkers like to stay in the deep water. The temperature there is more comfortable and more constant. However, a fish this size would starve to death in short order if it never left the depths. Here's a key to any large swimming predator: Big fish eat little fish! If you can't find the big fish, look for the little fish. Deep water is the bedroom for lake trout. It's not the kitchen. To eat, the fish has to travel to the shallow water, where small fish are more plentiful. Small fish don't hang out in 75 feet of water. They like to have structure, so they can hide—and their food is in shallow water, also. A small fish in open water is a larger fish's lunch.

The lake trout is a hunter—a small, freshwater great white shark. Be thankful that lake

FISH SEEKING THE SHADE OF A CANOE

trout don't grow bigger. If they did, they'd take a swimmer in a hungry gulp. You can dangle a line in their bedroom if you're using a different tackle system—it works for trollers and jiggers, but not for a fly caster. Mack are very opportunistic. They'll eat in the bedroom if something is available, but this would stretch fly gear too much.

When you use a fly rod, you have to fish where mack hunt. Fish in the kitchen, not in the bedroom. Look at the lake. Where is there an abundant supply of food? Better yet, if you were a small fish, where would you hide when so many predators were after you? You'd hide around fallen logs, rocks, boulders, and cliffs. Just as you do with stream fishing, look for seams. Where does the water suddenly get deep? Where are moss lines? Where do

streams enter the water? Is there a shelf between the deep and shallow water? Any of these areas are excellent places to start. You can see some structured areas by reading the water, but others you can't see. Most lakes you'll be fishing have maps of the bottom. Buy a map. Look at water depths, and look for shelves. Find a handy place where a laker can zip in, gulp down a few rainbow snacks, and swim back to its bedroom. Looking at a map, even if you've never seen the lake, is a good place to start. You can also talk to other anglers about how the bottom of the lake unfolds.

Lake trout patrol the shelves, the seams, the boulders, and the structure—in other words, the kitchen. A number of times at Fish Lake in Utah, which is one of my favorite places to fish on this earth, I've seen large trout swimming up and down the moss lines, looking for food. Like a bonefish fisherman in the Florida Keys, I often *hunt* for hunting lakers. When I see one, I cast a line. I stand up in my boat, moving in what I think is a likely area at nearly wakeless speed. I'm looking for fish that are 10 to 30 feet down. It stands to reason that you can fish this way only when the water is flat and there's enough light to see. I look for shadows and movement. I try not to take my eyes off the water. It's surprising what you see when you keep yourself attuned. There's a whole other world down there—one we rarely get a glimpse of. Big lakes aren't always cooperative beyond mid-morning, though. Once the wind comes up and there's any sort of chop, hunting fish is useless.

Besides helping me find a fish to cast at, hunting helps me locate areas where the fish are. I keep notes about where on the water I've seen lakers. Once the water gets a little rough and I can't see, I concentrate my efforts on these spots.

Water Temperature. Mack are sensitive to temperature. They can't stand extremes, and they like temperatures in the mid-50s. If the water gets over 60 degrees, it's not cozy. To keep themselves comfortable, they move about as you would expect, finding the right comfort zone for their bedroom. When eating, they will cruise into any water that has fish. After they have fed, they go back to the water they feel most at home in.

When the ice is off, mack move closer to shore. As the water warms up, they move back into deeper waters, where it's cooler. As fall approaches, they move back to shallower, warmer water. During the winter, when the water is iced over, they are very deep, where the water temperature is more constant.

While these fish are considered deep water creatures, during much of the year you'll find them in water that's only 20 to 30 feet deep. Watch the water temperature. Mack fly rodders who fish shallow water during the spring wear big smiles. During the first few weeks after ice-off, you'll sometimes find mack within casting distance of the banks. This is one of the best times to catch these elusive fish. They're in shallow waters because they like the temperature, but there's a double bonus for the angler. During the winter, the fish didn't move very much, because the cool water slowed their body processes down. The warm water of spring has brought on a tremendous hunger, and they're ready to food. They're trying to fatten up, so they hit everything in sight. To a lesser degree, the same sort of thing is true about the fall. In spring and fall, I usually focus my efforts on the same waters the mack normally hunt in. In addition to food, this water usually provides the right comfort requirements. The fish are very active.

The Spawn. This is one of the best times to hook really big lake trout. The spawn usually starts during the late fall in shallow, rocky shoal areas, where the water is about 10 to 25 feet deep. Mack like clear water. If you have to choose between two areas that seem about equal, go with the clearer water.

While fall is a great time to fish, it's often cold. The spawn occurs just before the ice. It's too cold for a float tube—at least it is to me—so a boat is a must. On some lakes you can wade, but it's usually pretty miserable. The wind is blowing, and it's hard to cast. I like to fish in the fall, but freezing to death isn't in my game plan. I fish only on nice autumn days, and then only from a boat.

Many lakes that host mack get a steady flow of diehards out for the big ones at this time of the year. Sometimes the water is rough, but you don't have to go that far from shore, so it's generally safe boating. I always keep an eye on the water and the sky. Don't take chances at this time of the year. Some lake trout waters are good-sized, like Flaming Gorge, and they can get rough. For your first time on a lake, go with someone who knows the water.

It's worth facing some cold, though, because the fish are aggressive during the spawn. Besides, fighting mighty fish with your fly gear warms you up, and each encounter gets you ready for another couple hours of casting. All you have to do is get your wet fly near a fish to get a response.

The fish favor rocky bottoms, so don't worry if you lose a few flies. If you're fishing correctly, this will happen. For most mack, you have to fish right off the bottom. If they are really aggressive, they'll come after your fly or see it suspended in the water when they're hunting. As a rule, though, they stay pretty close to the bottom, even when they're on the prowl. Your chances are best if you keep your fly within a foot of the bottom.

The female lays 700 to 800 eggs per pound of body weight, so a 30-pound fish might lay as many as 24,000 eggs. The female drops her eggs in the rocks, and the male fertilizes them. Even though there are no nests, mack feel threatened when something like your fly comes floating through the nursery. They're quick to gobble down the threat. What's important is getting your flies in front of the lake trout's nose, and that means having your fly right off the bottom. I could go on all day about flies, but let me say this: If you work the fly so it looks alive, almost anything you get to the fish will do the trick. I've enjoyed success with white and black jigs, streamers, and Muddler Minnows.

For this style of fishing, weight on the fly is an asset. Leaded jigs are very productive, even if they are a little clumsy to cast. I should also mention that you need a fast-sinking line and lots of backing. You won't cast much unless you're hunting, and even then you won't cast far. Remember that you are throwing a lot of weight. Otherwise you'll be feeding the line out and letting it sink. Jig it while it goes down and when you bring it up. I use about a four-foot, 10-pound test leader.

Work the fly delicately. You don't need the massive jerks you'll sometimes see among the bass rod-jigging set. Darting, careful movements are best. If the fly moves too much, it can scare away all but the most aggressive fish. It should dart up and down and back and forth like a small fish.

When lake trout take a fly, they pull rather than jerk. It's a long, steady tug. When you start to feel any sort of pull, set the hook. They spit out a fly very quickly, because they know almost at once that the fly is a fake. Your response time is critical. These tough-mouthed fish require well-honed hooks, and you really have to drive the point home. A fly rod isn't as stiff as a bass rod, so you must set the hook with passion. Lastly, it's almost impossible to land *any* big fish without a good net, so bring one along.

Whitefish

Whitefish don't get much respect. Many anglers consider them trash, but whitefish are the stars of winter fishing. They're a whole lot of fun, and they give you a nice break from the winter doldrums. Overall, they're underrated as a game fish.

If you're fishing for trout, sooner or later you'll accidentally latch onto a whitefish. They don't get very big—a three-pounder is good-sized. The state record in Utah is four pounds, seven ounces. As you'd expect, they are whitish to light brown, with silver sides. The face and lower jaw are blunt. The mouth looks a little like a sucker's. It's not a pretty fish, but it's not ugly, either.

You'll generally catch whitefish on small wet flies. You'll catch more in fall and winter than at any other time of the year. Many anglers throw them back without a thought. The truth is, in winter, when whitefish are easy to catch, they fight twice as hard as a trout. They seem to thrive on cold water—water that shuts the

Don't overlook whitefish. This specimen was caught on a #20 Griffith's Gnat in early spring.

trout action down until spring. A two-pound whitefish can be an exciting catch.

Not so long ago, few casters would go out just for whites, but we've changed our wicked ways. In the winter, I like to fish the rivers for whites and whatever trout I can hook. I fish them about the same way I fish for trout, because they eat many of the same foods.

If you want to increase your odds, use a light tippet and a #16-18 fly. Smaller seems to work better. The Pheasant Tail, Hare's Ear, and Chamois Nymphs are my favorites. I've also taken a few on Glow Bugs during the brown spawn. Many whitefish experts like dark flies, but I've had good luck with flies tied with reds and pinks. I use a strike indicator, and I try to get my fly deep so it will scoot across the bottom. Every now and then, a warm day sparks a winter hatch that brightens things up. This is usu-

ally a midge hatch, so be prepared with midge patterns and Griffith's Gnats in sizes #18-22. It's enjoyable to catch whitefish off the surface.

The whitefish is very tasty. It's a little bony unless it's filleted. It's good fried, but most of the time whitefish are smoked. Their flesh is a little oily, which makes them perfect for the smoker. In nearly all waters that I know of, taking a large batch from the stream (the limit is usually two or three times the limit for trout) doesn't hurt the population at all.

During winter months, when the water is too cold for hot trout action, try whitefish. They'll never replace trout, but they're tons of fun to fish for. They also school up. If you hook one, you're likely to hook another. Watch for whites at the bottom of riffles in a tailout pool. Fish the riffles, too, because they sometimes move into these waters to feed.

FIFTEEN

The Backpacking Fly Fisher

Lightweight Traveling Comfort

GETTING TO
THE SITE

L ET'S SAY YOU REALLY WANT TO GET BACK TO VIRGIN WATERS. You can parachute in with supplies, rent a horse or a pack train of mules, or maybe hire a Sherpa to carry your gear. Or you can strap on a backpack that holds everything you need to stay warm and dry, enough food to eat, and something comfort-able to sleep on. There are no roads, so you'll follow a narrow trail over hill and dale via foot power. And somewhere up there, you'll catch fish—lots of fish.

Backpacking with a fly rod often means good fishing. But it's a little more specialized, so I'd like to talk about the methods and gear you need to be aware of before you head off to the boonies. I also want to talk a little about backpacking itself, offering a few pointers for the seasoned pack-carrying veteran and a few pointers for the novice, so your trip will be more successful.

I've been on a few backpack trips from hell, and I hope you never have to endure one. Even Dante might recoil from some of my experiences. What makes them especially tragic is that most of the problems were avoidable. Here are some ghoulish highlights:

I split my food supply three ways on a 10-day hike, because my two confident, self-professed "world-class" angler companions thought they'd be living on fish while we hiked the Pacific Crest Trail.

I shared a tight mummy bag on a 13-degree night—*my* mummy bag—with another 185-pound male to keep him warm and alive in the frigid Alaska tundra. His bag got washed down the river when the water rose after a rainstorm.

I brought a ton of freeze-dried food, but we had nothing to boil water in. The person who was supposed to bring the cooking gear forgot it.

The list goes on, including having no matches, no rain gear, no spoons, and no warm coats in freezing weather. Most such problems can be prevented with a little forethought and planning. Most emergencies can be mitigated by cool thinking and carrying a few basic tools. So that your first adventure in the outback won't be your last, I want to go over some basics. The fishing is great, and I'd hate to see you miss out on it.

Fly Gear for the Backpacker

In addition to your regular backpacking gear, let's talk about the fishing gear you need for your trip into the great outdoors. You can't run to the local fly shop if you run out of leader or flies—it's the price you pay for solitude and great fishing.

A Travel Rod. The most obvious starting place is the rod. I'm a great proponent of the breakdown or travel rod. It's certainly the best choice when you pack. As I mentioned earlier, casters in the old days thought they lost sensitivity with breakdowns, but that's no longer the case with the better rods. There's little if any difference—none that I've noticed.

A breakdown rod is easy to pack. Most come in four pieces, allowing you to carry your rod in your pack. A rod that divides into two pieces will always be hanging out of your gear, or will force you to carry it in your hands. In either case, you're likely to break the rod.

Backpackers are often so weight-conscious that they trim the tops off tea bags or do other ridiculous things to cut back on the weight they carry. Many are tempted to leave the protective rod case at home. Don't. A little extra weight is a small price to pay to protect your rod.

The rod size you carry is predicated on where you want to go. However, unless you are fishing very small lakes and streams, I'd recommend a medium-weight rod (#6 or #7). Your rod will be stiff enough to cast a line in the strong afternoon wind that always seems to grace the high country. You'll also be able to

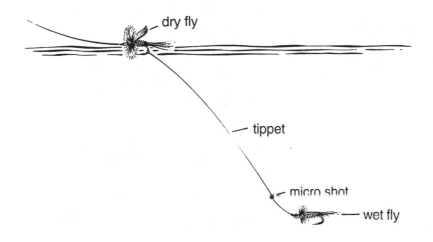

dry fly

tippet

micro shot

wet fly

A tip for fishing mountain lakes. Tie on a large dry fly. Tie a tippet to the shank of the dry fly, and attach a small wet fly with a micro shot. This way you can fish the surface and the deeper water at the same time.

cast a little farther, which might make all the difference on some waters.

Reel and Line. Some reels are considerably lighter than others. After a long hike, it could make a difference. If you're in a position to go light, do so. Otherwise, take whatever you have and be happy. To keep my reel (and line) clean and out of the trail dust, I always transport it in a Ziploc bag.

The fly line and backing are on the reel. There's generally no problem with line, but leader is a different story. If anything will run out, it's leader. It weighs nothing, but when you're in the high country, it seems to go fast. I always carry half a dozen nine-foot leaders. I can cut one down to make a wet leader if need be. I also carry extra tippet material, so I can mend my leader as it wears down. Instead of regular spools, I carry three types of line on a spool caddy. It's light, handy, and carries a lot of line.

Flies. Flies don't weigh anything, so I take a good selection. Mountain trout can be more finicky than a rich man's cat. I try to take sev-

eral hundred, which I can just about fit into one case. Attractors are my first choice. I want a good supply. My favorite generic choices are Adams, Royal Coachman, Wulffs, Black Gnats, and Yellow Hackles—my mainstays. It's important to have several in each size from #14 to #22. In fact, size is the critical factor. I've seen mountain cuts die for a #20 Black Gnat and absolutely ignore a #18.

Ants are a great casting staple, and trout love gulping them. Sometimes nothing works better. Bring flying ant patterns in a variety of sizes, and clip their wings as needed. Don't forget a selection of mosquitoes and caddis flies. Add a few Gray Hackle Peacock and White Miller patterns. Some attractors can be fished wet, but you'll need a few Scud, Hare's Ear, and Pheasant Tail patterns. Check your area for other local favorites.

Miscellany. I rarely bother to pack waders, unless they're absolutely necessary. The bulk is more troublesome than the weight. Thankfully, most mountain fishing can be done from the bank or by wading in shorts. However, wad-

For backcountry fishing trips, a good tent is a must.

ers are sometimes the only way to go. There are a number of lightweights on the market.

Don't forget odds and ends like clippers, floatant, and a hemostat or needle-nose pliers. It's also nice to have something to carry all your stuff in that still leaves room for a water bottle and a sandwich. A light vest is handy. A fanny pack, a knapsack, or a chest pack is useful. The key words are *light* and *roomy*.

Things That Go Bump in the Night

Sometimes during a fishing outing, things go bump . . . if not in the night, then during the day. It's not a perfect world out there. While encounters are infrequent, there are things out there that on rare occasion might take a bite out of you—bears and snakes.

The decision to carry a gun or some other means of defense when you're fishing is entirely personal. You might consider one of the new "assault" sprays, sometimes called anti-bear (and human) repellents.

Our friends in the wild kingdom are almost always more scared of us than we are of them. Most animals will run at the slightest hint of a human. However, every once in a while, this isn't the case.

Fishing with Bears. Bear encounters come to mind as most people's worst fear when fishing in the backcountry. If you fish in some of our national parks, in Alaska, in western Canada, or other bear-supporting wildlands, you may share a fishing hole with a bear. Because salmon offer such a rich food supply, the bruins in the north get really *big* and should be taken quite seriously.

Black bears and grizzly bears (and its cousins—the Kodiak, the mountain grizzly, the silvertip, the brown, the Alaskan brown, etc.) are awesome to watch—and dangerous. But if you're careful, they generally won't bother you.

Here are a few rules to follow when fishing in bear country:

1. Don't hike or fish alone.
2. Make lots of noise. Sing to yourself. Be very careful near water. The sound of the water will mask your noise and you could walk into a bear.
3. If bears are fishing at your favorite water, let it be. Give them some room and come back later. Don't try to move a bear.
4. Never shoot to kill unless a bear breaks your personal safety zone. Mine is about twenty yards. Give a warning shot first.
5. If you carry a gun, know how to use it well. Don't let it give you false confidence.
6. Always keep a clean camp. Don't leave food about. Never eat in your tent.
7. Check with local wildlife agencies for specific warnings and sightings, and to learn how to act if you do encounter a bear in the backcountry.

Fishing with Snakes. I hate snakes. But I'm not out to single-handedly blow them away either—unless they try to sink their fangs into my leg. I recognize that snakes have a place in our ecosystem. I just don't like them. I know that a poisonous snake will normally head for the nearest hole when I come along. I respect any snake that gets out of my way, and I'm pleased to let it go. Yet there have been a few occasions when a serpent didn't feel like moving, and I wasn't in a position to make a quick retreat and resume casting. On several occasions I've shot a diamondback or water moccasin. It's always best to prevent such situa-

Sometimes the best fishing spots for people are also the best fishing holes for bears. This stretch is bear-free at the moment, but it wasn't earlier.

tions, however. Here are a few tips for avoiding encounters of the viperous kind:

1. Always look where you intend to place your hands before you put them there.
2. Make noise when walking or fishing in snake habitat.
3. Stay alert. Watch where you're stepping.
4. Talk to local wildlife agencies before heading to snake-inhabited fishing spots.

Biking

Here's how to spend less time walking and more time fishing. By now, you know I'm a mountain biker. No chapter on backpacking would be complete without mentioning mountain biking, which goes hand in hand with backcountry travel. My mountain bike and I have been on a number of wonderful backcountry fishing and camping trips. On a bike, I can carry more stuff, and I get there quicker. I've used my bike in the summer when I was fishing in Yellowstone Park. Instead of walking from hole to hole, I'd hop on my mountain bike and ride to the next spot I wanted to fish. I calculated that I got 2½ extra hours of fishing one day because I was riding instead of walking. I may have looked silly on the road in my waders and vest, carrying a nine-foot rod, but the fish were worth it.

However you choose to travel to reach backcountry fishing, remember that you are a visitor there. Revel in the fishing, then leave no trace behind.

A mountain bike will allow you to extend your fishing range.

A List for the Compleat Fly Fishing Backpacker

ESSENTIAL EQUIPMENT
pack
sleeping bag
sleeping pad
hiking boots
tent or plastic tarp
canteen
cooking pot
mess kit
matches
small stove

CLOTHING
long pants
shorts
shirt
t-shirt
underwear
socks:
    four light pairs
    two heavy pairs
light jacket
heavier coat (if needed)
rain gear
down vest

FOODSTUFF
H_2O purification tablets, iodine, or pump
snacks:
    granola
    jerky
    gorp
    trail mix
    nuts
drinks:
    Kool-Aid
    Gatorade
    coffee
    hot chocolate
    teas
    soups
meals:
    freeze-dried
    MREs (Made Ready to Eat)
home foods (robbing the kitchen pantry)

FISHING GEAR
flies:
    Adams
    Coachman
    Wulffs
    Black Gnats
    Yellow Hackle
    ant patterns
    mosquito patterns
    caddis fly patterns
    Gray Hackle
    Peacock
    White Miller
    Scuds
    Hare's Ear
    Pheasant Tail
fly rod
fly rod case
reel
leaders
tippet materials
floatant
clippers
lead shot
strike indicator

MISC. MATERIALS
knife
mosquito netting
biodegradable soap
small first aid kit
medications
flashlight
batteries
bulbs
toilet paper
tissue
nylon cord
map of area
needle and thread
lighter
fire starter

EXTRAS

handgun
ammunition
pepper spray
camera
film
lenses
lens cleaner
small tripod
book
writing paper
snakebite kit

hand towel
trash bags
hand trowel
safety pins
signal mirror
Ziploc bags
aluminum foil
bug repellent
sunglasses
solar shower
Swiss Army knife
Gore-Tex socks

SIXTEEN

Tip a Canoe, the Float Tube, and You

Floating with Flies

WHEN YOU FIRST THINK OF FLY CASTING, YOU PROBABLY THINK OF WADING. You imagine the fly caster up to his or her thighs, the sun peeping over the edge of the snowcapped peaks, the mighty old-growth pines, and rays of lovely-warm goldenrod sunshine. You envision water as still as glass and as pure as crystal springs, and a light mix of vapors slowly recessing with the sunrise. Add perfect, 100-foot casts with candy-cane loops and a 5-pound lunker lightly slurping your exquisitely cast #20 dry fly.

Wading often does the trick, but not always. No matter how respectably you cast, no matter how perfect the beer-commercial setting, there are times when you'll have to get out farther, work the water from a different angle, or simply cover more water than you can on foot. When the fish are popping and you can't get to them, let alone work them properly, you'd sell your soul to have a shot at those fish.

To keep anglers from promising away their souls in a moment of fishing passion, floating devices were invented—float tubes, canoes, and rubber rafts. While a motorized craft might be handy, it isn't always practical for a caster, and motors are prohibited in many of the best fly waters. Portability and ease of transport are also considerations.

In any case, for the cost of a cheap, two- or three-horse trolling motor, you can buy a really good rod, a reel, a fly line, a float tube, and a reasonable canoe, and still have enough left to take the family out for lunch several times.

A float tube, a deluxe sort of inner tube that you propel using flippers, takes up almost no space at all, and it's very handy. It may be your first flotation purchase, along with a set of fins. You can cover a lot of water. A canoe is light and straps to almost anything. My 15-foot canoe can be handled alone, and I didn't have to get a bank loan to purchase it. A rubber raft is another handy way to reach good fishing. If I need a craft to fight the afternoon chop or wind, or if I have to stand to cast, I use a portable folding boat, such as a Porta-bote. My entire floating system cost quite a bit less than the smallest aluminum boat, a trailer, and a tiny trolling motor, and I can handle almost every fishing situation.

Above and Right: *Some fishing situations call for a boat. I've found the Porta-Bote to be an excellent tool. It's light enough to carry in one arm.*

Here are a few more reasons to take up floating:

1. To get away from the madding crowds.
2. To get away from the banks and growth-choked shorelines, so you can back cast.
3. You can properly work the shore-side feeding lanes without spooking the fish, because you're casting shoreward.
4. It's fun to be out on the water, and to be at one with the sensuous body of rocking waves.

5. You can stand in a boat, see the fish, and fish to them. It's called fish hunting.
6. Floating allows you to work a lot of pockets you couldn't otherwise fish.

Float Tubes: Doing it in a Donut

A donut is the best place to fish. You'll expand your fishing and get into unreachable waters. There's nothing like a "belly boat." I even use mine on very gentle rivers, fishing as I drift. The term "gentle river" is important—if I can't paddle upstream easily, it isn't gentle.

When I first started tubing, I paid a lot and didn't get much. The tube had a flimsy nylon shell. Now the prices for float tubes have come down, and you get more for your dollar. For just under $100, you can get a good system. The zippers are well-sewn, and the nylon is thicker. There's a carrying strap, lots of pockets, and a double tube for safety's sake.

Even in the summer, I like to wear a heavy wader, because I get cold if I'm in the water for very long. I like a stocking wader with slipover fins. Displacing little water, you can fish effectively. With a sinking tip line, another world awaits you.

My first experience in a tube happened in Yellowstone Park a decade ago. It was June 15, and cutthroat fishing had just opened up. I slipped into the waters off Gull Point without knowing what to expect. Almost at once, I started to catch fish on a Green Leech pattern, not noticing that the wind was starting to pick up. It wasn't a big wind, just a steady breeze. By the time I'd

Sometimes it's you, the morning, and your float tube. It adds up to real fishing magic.

hooked and released five good cuts, I was ¾ of a mile from the shore.

"I gotta get back," I muttered. I made a little headway against the stiff breeze. With a good kick, I was progressing slowly but surely. Not wanting to waste my time, I cast and stripped back the line. The shore was a little closer.

SLAM! I set the hook with my trusty rod and struggled with a Goliath cut. The trout took off the for deep, and I palmed my reel. I was into my backing. What a fish! What a fighter! By the time I released it, I realized I'd lost whatever headway I'd made, and the wind had shifted slightly to the east. I kicked as hard as I could, but I couldn't make Gull Point or the other shore near Bridge Bay. I was floating east,

and there was quite a chop on the water by now. Whitecaps occasionally obscured my view of the shore.

To make a long story short, I tumbled into Pelican Bay a few hours later, awfully tired and needing a Coke. I scared the hell out of two lazy buffalo and a few elk when I climbed up the steep bank. I stashed my tube and rod in the brush and walked in stocking feet to the nearest road. I was cold and hungry but feeling good, now that it was over. I flagged down a driver who didn't seem to mind my shoelessness.

I realized a few things after my adventure. First, I was lucky to be in one piece. The wind can do strange things to you when you're bouncing over the water at its mercy. Had it

FLOATING TOO FAR OUT

blasted in another direction, I could have been walking my way out of some serious wilderness or saying hello to a smiling grizzly. What if my tube had developed a leak? I'd be fish food or mighty frozen.

I've learned my lesson. I now have a second flotation device on my tube. I wear a personal flotation device (a good life jacket), and I carry a small Ziploc bag containing a candle and waterproof matches. Another bag holds granola bars, nuts, and dried fruit. I also carry a light rain suit and a light pair of canvas shoes, so I don't have to walk in my stocking feet. I've become more careful of wind currents and big waters. I stay closer to shore, so I can hightail it back in if conditions look rough.

Getting Tubed. Unless you use the U-tube style of float, which conveniently opens at one end but costs quite a bit more than the inner tube float, you'll need a little bit of practice getting in and out of the tube, so you don't end up on your rear end. Even with practice, you'll take a tumble every once in a while. Walking in awkward fins, gripping a tube, struggling with your rod, your net, and other gear is cumbersome to say the least. Getting in and out of the tube—not to mention putting on your fins, then waddling in and out of the water—takes some orchestrated practice.

But first things first. Always double-check your tube's air pressure just before you use it. Also check the safety air bladder that is standard in most tubes. And it's not a bad idea to check the stitching in the fabric every so often. I was fishing with my friend Gary on Fish Lake once when I heard a loud four-letter word

and a sort of *kerr-plop*. I looked in Gary's direction and saw a strange sight. His head was bobbing up and down where the seat strap in his float was supposed to be. His right arm was stretched above his head, with his expensive fly rod in his hand. His left hand was grasping the side of the tube.

Gary viewed this as a sign from God that he needed to go on a serious diet. In any case, taking a cold dip was a surprisingly perfect way to ruin a great trip for fall rainbows. He was pretty chilly, and his clothes were wet. Nevertheless, Gary feels that his personal flotation device kept him from going under any farther than he did. After I towed him into shore, trying not to laugh once I found out everything was okay, we discovered that a few years of use and too much sun had rotted out the stitch-

Some float tubes are U-shaped, making them easier to get in and out of. The skirt on this tube is useful—if you drop a fly, it won't be lost.

ing and the fabric in the seat strap. Since that time, I've periodically checked my float's fabric and stitching. The experience suggests that a good personal flotation device (life jacket) can save your life and your fly rod. If your tube's stitching looks weak, have it restitched immediately.

I've tried every way in the world to make the process of getting into a tube easier. But let's face it. You're walking like a duck. You're walking backwards. You can't see your feet, and you're clinging to a giant Cheerio. While there are a hundred ways to skin a cat, a backward foot entry is the best method I've found to get in the water sort of safely. It goes something like this:

1. Find a clear, smooth place as close to the water as you can. Make sure there are no big rocks around—or even medium-sized ones.
2. Put the fins about three feet from the water. The heels should face the water.
3. Put the tube down in back of the fins, so the front of the tube is almost touching the heels. The tube may be partly in the water. Some people put the tube *over* the fins, but this makes the process even more awkward. Again, a flat place makes this whole thing easier.
4. Set your rod and any other gear you aren't wearing aside. The gear should be far enough away so you don't step on it, but close enough so you won't trip getting to it.
5. Pull the tube up around you (most have handles), and hold it at about knee-level. Step into your favorite fin first and secure it. Depending on the kind of fins you have,

**In a tube, you can play a fish on lighter tackle,
because there isn't much to get hung up on.**

A canoe is a great fishing tool that's fun for the entire family.

you may or may not need to set your float down in order to secure the fins to your stocking foot or boot. Then secure the other fin.

6. Grab your rod and gear, hold your tube, and take small, careful, short, backward steps into the water. When you're in deep enough water, sit down and paddle.

Tip a Canoe

I'll never be a brilliant canoeist. I've taken some unplanned baths when I've tried to stand up, or when I've had a great fish and tumbled over the edge of the canoe trying to unhook it.

Happily, though, it's been a long while since I've dumped a canoe. At my ripe old age, I've come to grips with canoes. I no longer stand up and look for mule deer on an adjacent slope or lean over too far to unhook a fish. Once these lessons sunk in, I caught more fish and quit going in headfirst. I also notice that my fishing buddies are more likely to go out on the water with me.

A canoe is an excellent tool—a traditional way to lay your line upon the water in style. Unlike a regular boat, it can be very affordable. You can spend as much or as little as you'd like. A good general canoe serves the caster on a budget. I've put my 15-footer through a lot. It's not specialized for any one sort of water, but it's very tough. It even survived falling off my truck.

If you're really into canoeing and don't mind spending a bit more money, you might consider a number of other, more specialized canoes. They perform with precision. Your local canoe distributor can help you find the right boat for your activities.

In a canoe, you can cover plenty of water, carry a lot of stuff, and enjoy the journey. I live like a king when I'm canoeing in the Wind River Mountains, fishing my way across a lake, then portaging to the next to fish some more.

On large waters, you have to be careful of the wind and the chop. Mornings and evenings are the best canoe times unless you can find a quiet, secluded bay. If you start to get much of a wave, you'll need to head for shore. No fish is worth a dunking. Many canoes are made for white water, but I'm not an expert. If the rapid looks too rough, I'll cheat the wave by going through at the edges or by portaging my canoe.

Motorboats

I've done quite a bit of casting from motorboats. It can be a successful way to go. However, a boat that's too big takes the fun out of it, at least for me. Almost every year, I head to southern Oregon and cast for landlocked trout on Klamath Lake. I literally hunt for the fish and cast to them. I'm fine in a small boat. But if it's too large, I scare the fish more easily and I can't cast accurately.

It's probably obvious that I like an open boat with little to get hung up on. If you have to stand and make long casts into the wind, the less there is to get hung up on the better. You want to be able to cast freely in all directions.

Whether you fish from a float tube, a canoe, or another type of boat, you'll find that floating will broaden your fly fishing capabilities—and double your fun.

SEVENTEEN

Odds and Ends

Considering "Stuff"

MODERN FLY FISHING

I'D LIKE TO GO OVER SOME FLY FISHING-RELATED ODDS AND ENDS THAT I SIMPLY CALL *STUFF*. You'll be interested in this stuff sooner or later, if you're not already. As with any sport, there are little tidbits that most experienced fly casters learn through experience, stuff you assimilate randomly over a period of time. To shorten your learning curve and save you some headaches, I want to discuss a few things that will ease your life as a caster. Knowing some of this will help you catch fish indirectly, if not directly.

What They'll Sell You. Most stuff has a price tag attached to it, and you may have to learn whether it's a good or bad buy after the fact. I usually learn the hard way. I know you aren't made of dollars, so let's see if we can save you money, time, and aggravation.

181

This passion we call fly casting often gets consuming. Everything you'll want for birthdays, Christmas, or vacations will be fly casting related. Because we're so passionate about our sport, we're sometimes blinded. Frankly, casters are a little gullible, too. Because most of the fly fishing people we know are so nice, and because the fly fishing folks we bump into on the river are so amicable, we think everyone and everything associated with our sport is equally guileless.

Think again. Our love for casting translates into big consumer bucks, and a lot of concerns are trying to sell us something. There are a lot of hands out. Some products or services are really worthwhile, and merit our consideration. Other stuff looks nice, but is practically useless. Some things are a total rip-off.

Life is full of promises and lies. The biggest promise and the worst lie most casters tell is, "I'll clean the garage out next week when the spawn is over. I really will." The promises made by many of the folks on Madison Avenue are less sincere and no less a lie. Advertising types are interested in selling and not much interested in fishing. In the name of creating a good ad campaign, many promoters make outrageous claims that most normal folks would call black lies. Somehow, when we put on the fishing mantel we become slow-moving targets with bull's-eyes for the ad guys in funny-looking $700 suits who market a barrage of allegedly necessary fishing products. Again, many products and services are useful and value-laden. Many are not.

I'm the perfect authority, because I've bought stuff in both categories. According to my wife, I buy everything advertised in every fishing magazine sooner or later. She's never let me forget the Rambo knife I put a rush order on a few years ago. The manufacturer promised it would do everything from skinning white-tailed deer to unplugging toilets. Actually, it now functions quite nicely as a backup soft-butter knife in our trailer. It also serves as a reminder to spend money wisely.

From experience, I can tell you that once you get into this phenomenal sport, you'll eventually want every piece of fly fishing gear ever made. Until you get yourself in control, you'll spend as if your self-worth was directly related to accumulation. But dollars don't grow on trees, and besides, you'd need to build a second home, a large shed, or an expanded basement to hold a fraction of the gear you might think you need. At our house, we call our basement the Rambo Room. All the stuff I've bought but don't dare throw out because I paid good money for it is tossed into a big pile and forgotten.

You probably have other money demands besides fishing stuff—like food for your family, insurance premiums, braces, and in-line skates. As a solid, middle-class sort, I know the financial constraints most of us face. There are a few well-off fly casters who can get it all, but most casters have budgets (and are known to ignore them). With this in mind, let's talk about some of the useful gear you really don't need when you're starting out but might want later on.

A net is essential if you respect your fish. Make sure you choose a net with a cotton basket.

Nets. A net should be at the top of your list of not-quite-essential but really important items. I like carrying a net because it makes landing fish easy and safe—for me and for the fish. A net can be a hassle when you're trudging through the brush, but it's a wonderful convenience otherwise. Unless you get really good at grabbing fish out of the water, a net will improve your landing average by 50 percent or more.

Because fly fishers often use light tippet, there's a lot of strain on the end of the line. This is especially true when the fish is in close. A fish that's being reeled in gets a sudden burst of energy when it sees a big human a few feet away. This puts an added strain on the line. With a net, you can usually scoop the fish right up. You don't have to let it make another run. You net it before it has a chance to realize how scary the situation is and bolt to the farthest corner of the pool.

Nets are easier on fish—especially if you have a net with a soft cotton basket, which is the only kind you should use. Using your net, you can scoop up the fish and release it before it gets completely worn out. It's easier on a fish to thrash about in soft cotton string than it is to endure a caster's too-hard squeeze. Once the fish is in the net, you can grasp it firmly but gently. The supple strings help hold the fish. With a good grip, you can easily remove the fly and quickly release the fish. A net speeds up the process, getting the fish back into the water with less stress.

Nets are a big plus in cold weather. You don't have to submerge your tender hand in the icy water. The drier you stay, the warmer you stay. It's no fun to have your hands glazed over with ice.

There are a thousand nets on the market. At all costs, avoid those with a nylon basket. Nylon is abrasive and can be hard on your fish. Most aluminum nets and the cheapest wooden models have nylon baskets. Look for a soft cotton net, even though you'll have to pay more. You can buy several aluminum nets with fish-killing nylon baskets for the price of a net with a cotton basket, but consider your net an investment in fish futures. The softer the basket, the more fish you'll save.

I usually can't afford custom gear, but I've found a net maker who makes beautiful hardwood nets that fit my hand and have the softest cotton baskets I've seen. His nets are so well-crafted that you'd feel good about hanging them on the wall, yet they're tough enough to last in the field for years. I purchased a net three years ago, and it's seen days and days of use. In fact, it's featured in nearly all the netting pictures in the book.

The advantages of a custom net are many. You are dealing with a craftsman who fly fishes, so you have a product that works and can be fixed if something goes wrong. You can pick your favorite style and wood. But the big plus is that you can have the handle cut for your

hand. Shoes and gloves aren't one-size-fits-all, so why should net handles be generic? Another nice thing is that custom nets don't cost any more than those you'd order out of a catalog. For a little more than you'd pay for a good fly line, you can have a net that feels good in your hand and lasts for years.

Equipment for Winter Fishing. By now you know that fly fishing isn't just a three-season sport. There are fish to be caught in the winter, and some of them are *big* fish. The trick is to avoid freezing while you're doing it. I've mentioned that I take a thermos of Postum and hang it around my neck. Every so often, I take a drink of warm liquid. This helps keep me warm from the inside out. There are a few things you can do to keep yourself warm from the outside in.

First of all, wear a hat. Keep your head warm. Most of my coats have hoods on them, and I use them, but a hood alone isn't enough. A stocking cap or a cap with earflaps is better. Yes, they look dumb, but the trout don't care, and you can stay out twice as long as the stylish guy who has icicles dangling from his ear lobes.

I've tried every sort of glove arrangement ever marketed, but none seems perfectly suited to fly fishing. In the winter, you're usually fishing wet flies. The pickup is very subtle, even with a strike indicator. It's really important that you feel your rod at all times, or you'll miss a lot of strikes. For me, a glove hampers the process. At the same time, it's hard to set the hook with a frozen, numb hand. I often use wool, fingerless gloves or neoprene gloves. But my hands still get cold.

To keep them warm, I use solid fuel hand warmers, one in each pocket. When I start to get numb, I switch my rod to the other hand and grab the warmer for a minute or two until I can feel again. If the weather is really cold, I'll burn both sides of the solid fuel stick, increasing the heat output. I go through more fuel, but it's worth it. Hand warmers and fuel sticks are inexpensive and can be purchased anywhere. I don't like lighter fuel hand warmers. I'm always afraid one is going to go *boom* in my pocket and ruin a day's fishing. The only thing I don't like about solid fuel heaters is the pungent smell they exude if they're lit in a vehicle or indoors. Outdoors, the smell is hardly noticeable. The disposable, emergency hand warmers sold in sporting goods stores also work moderately well.

There are other tricks to staying warm. The most important one is making sure your waders don't leak. Next important is using the thickest neoprene chest waders you can find. What do you wear underneath your waders? This isn't the time for Levis. When it's cold, I start with a thin pair of polypropylene underwear. Next, I like a pair of thick fleece pants—the material used to be called polar fleece, but now everyone has a different name for it. It's a miracle fabric. It feels like wool, but it weighs a lot less. It stays warm when it's damp, and it dries in no time.

I used to wear a pair of thick sweats, but sweats aren't much good if they get damp, and they don't wick perspiration. I like really thick fleece—the stuff really works when it's cold. If it's really cold, I'll throw on a pair of long johns and wool pants over the fleece.

I like to wear two or three pairs of socks, but if I bulk up too much, I have a hard time getting my wading shoes on. I often wear a thin polypropylene pair and a thick wool pair. If it's really cold, I'll use two medium-thick pairs over the polypropylene. It's a snug fit, but I can honestly say I've never had uncomfortable toes unless my feet got wet.

I like to layer the rest of my stunning outdoor wardrobe with an assortment of warm, well-used clothing. I always wear a polar fleece jacket over a heavy wool shirt. Then comes a down vest. In the canyons where I fish, wind can be a factor, so I'll wear a windbreaker. Next, I'll wear a big, bulky sweater or a winter parka.

Sometimes a guided trip means floating. With a guide, you can spend your time fishing instead of hassling with gear and logistics.

It takes me forever to get dressed. I'm so bulky I can't walk very far. I look dumb. But I'm warm, and I can thus stay on the water for a long time. In late November and December, the fishing is good in my part of the Rockies. The weather can get down to the teens, with a 20-mph wind. Except for my hands and face, I stay toasty. When I'm this bulked up, I always fish with a friend. I don't wander too far from my Bronco in case I need to get back to it quickly, and I don't wade in tricky water.

Guides and Packaged Fishing Trips. It can make sense to book a packaged fishing trip or a guide. Maybe you don't know the area or

the waters well. Perhaps it's wild country, and thus is unforgiving to pilgrims. You may not have time to plan the trip on your own. The area may be sewn up by a concession. Perhaps you enjoy having someone take you to the best waters, prepare your meals, and make lodging arrangements, so all you have to do is fish. A package may be cheaper than setting the trip up yourself. Or you may not know how to do it by yourself.

For whatever reason, a packaged tour with guides is often a nice way to go. If you don't know the water or the runs, a guide can show you what to do and where to fish, and then you can branch out on your own. It can take the guesswork out of a trip. I've been on some really good guided trips and some not-so-good guided trips. At their best, guided trips can be fishing heaven. At their worst, they can be the fishing vacation from hell. Most of the guides I've booked have done their job, and I've been pleased. But a few have left a sour taste in my mouth.

My fishing trip from hell took place in Saskatchewan in June of 1985. It was the worst nine days of my life. Mickey Mouse and a class of first-graders would have done a better job as guides, cooks, and organizers. The guides were drunk; the equipment was broken down; the food was awful; the tackle, lures, and flies supposedly provided were nonexistent; the cabins leaked; there was no toilet paper or soap within 50 square miles. I could go on and tell you about the *bad* things, but I won't. Except I'll mention that the drinking water was not safe, and I caught a case of giardia. The list goes on.

I could have prevented all this by doing some homework. I found this outfit at an outdoor show in Salt Lake City, where they were booking trips for the next summer. The low price should have been the first indication that something was wrong. Now, low price alone isn't reason to shy away. Some outfits offer low prices and do a good job. Perhaps they've cut a deal with the airlines. Maybe you share in some of the work, or you stay in tents instead of cabins. There are a number of ways a guide can keep the cost down. However, low price can also mean hidden costs or diminished services.

The first thing you need to do is find out what you're getting and exactly what the package costs. Most of us are stretched by the price of the trip alone—any extra costs need to be factored in from the start. You can't add charges to a credit card that's already tapped out. Are there hidden motel bills? Is there a rental car fee or an extra air taxi fee? How much extra are the license and shipping if you bring a fish home? Don't just look at the pictures, listen to the sweet talk, and write a check. Before you part with bucks, know exactly what they expect of you and what you can expect of them. Ask for a list of references and call a few people on the list. Ask those people if there were any hidden costs. Find out how well they thought the guides did their job. Was the package everything it was cracked up to be?

The price of a few phone calls can save you a bundle. My trip from hell was put together fast, and I just got sucked in. It was my fault for not doing my homework. I should have called a few people and asked about food, cabins, fishing, and conditions. I've since made it a rule that, before booking a trip, I call at least five former clients.

If the reference list contains only half a dozen names and they all look like relatives, be suspicious. Do a little investigating.

If I'm at an outdoor show, I'll ask one outfit why they are better than another. Do a little investigating. How long has the guide or the outfit been in business? Check out several outfits. If one offers really low prices, is there a reason? Take the time to ask all the important questions. If you aren't getting the right answers, take your business elsewhere.

Videotapes. Watching instructional fishing videos can help you become a better fly fisher. There are tapes for everyone from the beginner to the expert. Many fly shops and video stores rent them, but you can also purchase your own copy. Many tapes are made for casters by casters. You'll get information that will really help you—and you'll see plenty of exciting fish caught and lost. I like knowing that even the experts bust a few tippets now and then. These videos are a great way to learn and a great way to spend a stormy afternoon.

Bags. What do bags have to do with fly fishing? Look around the next time you see a bunch of casters. They're involved in a gear-oriented sport, and they need something to carry the gear in. What do they carry it in? Bags. The folks who make casting equipment have learned that there is a great market for bags. Fly fishing is the most bag-oriented sport there is.

You'll use bags when you travel to fish. You'll use them when you're going to and from the river, and for storing stuff. I always keep bags of fishing gear in my Bronco, so I can stop whenever a section of water looks right. If I'm going on a long trip, I pull a few bags out of the closet, filled with more fishing stuff, and I'm out the door in minutes. The hatch waits for no man, and a brown trout waits for no woman.

You'll likely tote your gear in soft-sided bags—luggage that is light, easy-to-carry, and stuffable. When you buy it, make sure you get the right kind. There aren't any perfect bags, but there are a number of really good ones out there. A few midsized bags are easier to carry and easier to use than one large one. Unless you have a specific need for a really large bag, I wouldn't use one. Some feel there are advantages to flying on commercial planes with one big bag. They think airlines are less likely to lose a large one. I'm not sure. I've found that airlines can lose just about anything.

As a quick aside, a backpack makes a good bag when you're flying and you want to keep everything together. You can't load it as full as a big bag, but you can pack it, and it's meant to be carried. Transporting it isn't a problem. Backpacks are tough, and the frame protects them during the handling/transportation process.

When you buy a bag, you get what you pay for. There are cheap bags, moderately priced bags, and expensive bags. While the cheap bags may work for storing stuff in your car or your fishing closet, they shouldn't be used when you're traveling. Why would you want to send off hundreds or thousands of dollars' worth of gear in a $15 bag? The conveyer belt at your local airport could trash it in a second, and you'd find reels and lines scattered all over the place. You've got valuable stuff. Treat it well.

A good bag costs money, but paying a lot doesn't mean you're getting a good bag. I like to check all zippers to ensure that they're high-quality and that they work properly. Zippers are the first thing to go. I check the stitching next, to be sure places that get a lot of wear are reinforced. The bag should be double-stitched; the tread should be high-quality; and the zipper should be well-sewn. I want everything stitched well because no matter how carefully I pack, I inevitably overstuff, stressing the sides and the seams. Next I look at the handles and imagine what the bag will feel like if it's overpacked. Are the handles sewn in well? What is the bag made of? How waterproof is it? Is the bottom reinforced?

Notice how the bag is organized. I have a gear bag that I'm fond of because it has a lot of pockets and a gear storage place that's perfect for reels.

I suppose there is no perfect bag for every situation, but I'll keep searching.

As a final comment on odds and ends, *stuff* should be a means to an end, not the end itself. The first job of a fly caster is to catch fish— and to catch them with grace, style, and respect. You don't want to be so burdened with gear, and decisions about gear, that this sport ceases to be fun.

Well, I hope to see you on the water sometime. Come over for a chat, and we'll talk about the one that got away. (I'll likely need to borrow one of your flies.) In the meantime, catch lots of fish and have a great time casting.

Tight Lines!

If You Want to Learn More . . .

Videos

Scientific Anglers has a great series of fishing and fly tying videos. They are well made and very informative. Look for them at your local fly fishing shop.

Books and Magazines

Basic Fly Tying, by Ed Koch and Norm Shires (Stackpole Books), is a simple, no nonsense discussion of the basics of tying. A good book for someone who has never tied.

The Compleat Angler, by Izaak Walton, is a must for every caster's collection. A book steeped in tradition and good sense. Read it!

Fly Fishing Made Easy: A Beginner's Guide, by Michael Rutter and Dave Card (Globe Pequot Press), is an overview of fly casting.

Fly Fishing the Tailwaters, by Ed Engle (Stackpole books). An excellent book on fishing tailwater streams for the intermediate and advanced caster.

Fly Tying: Adventures in Fur, Feathers, and Fun, by John McKim (Mountain Press), is a good introduction to tying flies.

Fly Tying For the Compleat Idiot: Crafting the Perfect Fly, by Michael Rutter and Kirby Cochran (Wind River Press, July 1995).

The Illustrated Encyclopedia of Fly-Fishing, by Silvio Calabi (Henry Holt and Company), is an excellent reference for fly casters. It's a complete A to Z of terminology, tackle, and techniques.

McClane's New Standard Fishing Encyclopedia, edited by A. J. McClane (Holt, Rinehart and Winston), is the best standard work on fish and fishing ever compiled. It is a must for every serious angler.

Selective Trout, by Doug Swisher and Carl Richards (Nick Lyons Books). This is an excellent book for the intermediate to expert caster.

Western Fly Tying Manual, by Jack Dennis (Snake River Books), is a straight forward fly tying manual.

The Flyfisher, The Magazine of the Federation of Fly Fishers. A quarterly publication.

INDEX